WHICH WAY, LORD?

WHICH WAY, LORD?

Exploring Your Life's Purpose
in the Journeys of Paul

ROB FUQUAY

ENLARGED-PRINT EDITION

UPPER
ROOM BOOKS®
NASHVILLE

Library of Congress Cataloging-in-Publication Data

Names: Fuquay, Rob, author.

Title: Which way, Lord? : exploring life's purpose in the journeys of Paul /
Rob Fuquay.

Description: Nashville : Upper Room Books, 2017.

Identifiers: LCCN 2016048225 | ISBN 9780835817035 (enlarged print) |
ISBN 9780835817042 (mobi) | ISBN 9780835817059 (epub)

Subjects: LCSH: Bible. Epistles of Paul—Criticism, interpretation, etc. |
Life—Biblical teaching. | Life—Religious aspects—Christianity.

Classification: LCC BS2655.L53 F87 2017 | DDC 227/.06--dc23

LC record available at https://lccn.loc.gov/2016048225

Printed in the United States of America

To

SARAH WILKE,
my sister-in-law,
a Paul-like leader
whose courage, faith, and love
have blessed the church around the world

CONTENTS

LOCATING YOUR STARTING POINT

What does it benefit you to know how beautiful a creature a human is if you ignore humanity's purpose, which is clearly to worship God in order to live eternally?

—Martin Luther

For everything, absolutely everything, above and below, visible and invisible . . . *everything* got started in [Christ] and finds its purpose in him.

—Colossians 1:16, THE MESSAGE

First there was Saul. And then there was Paul. I like the fact that the apostle Paul went by another name before he began his mission to the Gentiles. That makes it easy to distinguish between the "before" and "after"—not that the two didn't have a lot in common. Both acted with a singular devotion to the God of Israel. Both knew scripture backward and forward. And both sought purpose in their daily lives.

But Saul the Pharisee persecuted Christ-followers and was present at the stoning of one of Jesus' original disciples. Paul the Apostle, a dynamic communicator, advanced the cause of Christ. What happened? How did Saul become Paul?

The pivot point lies on the road to Damascus from Jerusalem. As Saul travels on it, the startling appearance of light from heaven halts him. Speaking directly to Saul, Jesus makes himself clear: *You need to choose another way.* Talk about an attention getter!

At this moment, the Saul-to-Paul transformation begins. But now comes the hard part. Paul has to figure out which way.

Isn't that the predicament we all face? As Christians, we yearn to live out God's purpose for our lives, but how do we know for certain which way to go?

This book aims to help you understand God's direction for your life. Your guide for this journey will be Paul, the globe-trotting hero of early church history. Along the way you'll gain more than an introductory insight into the background, education, experiences, writing, and theology of this man who changed the world.

Yet more than the *whats* of his life, we'll examine the *whys*. We won't simply look at where he went and what he said. We want to know how Paul got where he did. What determined his direction, and, more importantly, what determined his *changes* in direction? Did Paul have a pipeline to God that average people like you and me don't have? Or does Paul have something to teach us about what it means to discern God's guidance and direction for our lives? This study will answer those questions.

A lot of books about Paul and about the subject of finding purpose flood the market. There's also no end to life coaches, secular psychologists, and social commentators weighing in on this matter. But this book approaches the topic solely from a faith perspective.

That perspective also helps us understand what separated Saul from Paul. Remember that both sought purpose in their lives. But only Paul sought God's purpose as made manifest in Jesus Christ. The difference lay in the direction.

Saul's purpose grew out of intellect and knowledge of scripture, his certainty of what God wanted from him and, above all, of following the letter of religious law. Perhaps he believed his obedience would earn him God's love and acceptance. But let's face it: When you're persecuting people in the name of God, something is amiss. I'd like to think that part of Saul evidenced an openness to trying a different direction by the time Christ appeared.

Once transformed, Paul turned Saul's belief system upside down. Love eclipsed the law. God's acceptance wasn't the goal—it was the starting point! Knowing God's love made manifest in Jesus Christ became the primary motivating force of Paul's life, as it is intended to be for all of us.

Paul not only put his faith in Jesus Christ, but he also believed Christ put his faith in him—again, as Christ does in all of us. This is key: From this reciprocal faith flows the wellspring for doing good, being useful, and achieving a sense of fulfillment. In other words, for purpose.

Paul didn't arrive at this realization in a day, a month, or even a year. In fact, he spent several years discerning this new understanding of faith. (We'll explore the significance of this phase of his life in chapter 1.) When Paul's first call finally came, he set off to serve a growing Christian congregation in Antioch of Syria. If you believe God has a sense of irony, then this story won't let you down: Among the members of this church reside some of the very Christ-followers whom Paul had persecuted in his former life. What could have gone terribly wrong instead turned into an expression of Christ's love that would be seared on Paul's heart. The Christians of Antioch embraced him as a leader, and he experienced the warmth of their fellowship.

Here we evidence the power of community that plays a crucial role in Paul's transformation. Christianity doesn't operate in a vacuum. It flourishes when we share God's love with one another, which ignites further transformation in ourselves and in others.

The transforming power of community is not Paul's story alone. John Wesley, the father of Methodism, shares a similar one.[1] By the time Wesley boarded a ship in 1735 to come to America, he was an up-and-coming preacher steeped in religious study who spread the gospel of personal holiness and righteousness. No doubt he intended to live out God's purpose. Yet an experience on that voyage led him to acknowledge a lack in his own faith.

When a storm raged on the Atlantic one night, Wesley's English companions screamed and cowered; surely Wesley felt fearful himself. But he marveled at a group of German Christians called Moravians who worshiped and calmly sang hymns while the storm raged. What accounted for their composure? One Moravian explained to Wesley that the group was "not afraid to die"—strange words to a man who believed he had to be sanctified, that he had to live a holy life, before God would accept him.[2]

Like Paul's moment of reckoning on the road to Damascus, the episode began a lengthy period of discernment for Wesley that led him to learn more from the Moravians. Upon his arrival in Georgia, he sought out a Moravian pastor who posed the question: "Do you know Jesus Christ?"

"I paused," Wesley wrote in his journal, recounting the conversation, "and said, 'I know He is the Saviour of the world.' 'True,' replied he, 'but do you know He has saved you?'"

Wesley wrestled with this question even as he struggled to bring people to Christ. Two years later he departed Georgia, depressed and defeated. "I who went to America to convert others," he wrote, "was never myself converted to God."[3] Imagine his desperation at this point. How many times do you think he was driven to his knees to pray, in so many words, Which way, Lord?

Back in London Wesley accepted an invitation one evening from the Moravians to attend a religious meeting. It was there, while listening to Martin Luther's preface to Romans, that Wesley felt his heart "strangely warmed."[4] *God touched his heart!* I'd call that another attention getter.

Wesley realized he didn't have to *earn* God's acceptance. He'd found the starting point to a new, God-inspired direction. His purpose grew from God's love, and he lived out that purpose by taking the message of this boundless love to his parishioners. Eventually, Wesleyan theology would spread throughout the world.

I find it hard to believe that either the apostle Paul or John Wesley would have found his purpose without the influence of strong faith communities, which makes their stories my story too.

I grew up in Winston-Salem, North Carolina, and was baptized as an infant in a Methodist church. My mother, a registered nurse, often drew Sunday shifts so my family grew out of the habit of attending church by the time I got to elementary school.

Fifth grade was a tough year for me. My teacher assigned me to a desk between two troublemakers, and she unfairly lumped us all together in her mind. My confidence disappeared. My grades took a nosedive. I felt lost. My parents kept asking me what was wrong, but my answers all sounded like excuses.

Then in sixth grade, my family moved to another neighborhood, and I changed schools. Suddenly, I realized I'd been given a new chance to figure out who I was and who I wanted to be. A neighbor invited me to a Boy Scout meeting that met in the basement of a Methodist church. Since most of the scouts were active in the church, I soon followed. This was my first real exposure to the gospel—in the midst of a church community that made me feel like family.

But don't think I was now on the fast track to becoming a preacher. No way. I wanted to be a lawyer. I'd made a pact with my best friend to be partners in our own firm one day. My Plan B was to be a basketball star.

In ninth grade, I took a career test that supposedly identified occupations that lined up with my strengths. I can't remember my top option, but I'll never forget what I saw at the very bottom: minister. I certainly agreed with that, though I was disappointed by the occupation ranked second to last: attorney. But truth be told, I was just fourteen and in no great hurry to figure out what to do with the rest of my life.

Around the same time, I started working on my God and Country Award in scouting. One requirement involved shadowing my pastor. I went with him on visits to hospitals and calling on members in their homes. I remember how energized I felt when I finished those visits. Yet that feeling didn't come close to comparing to the one I got from another assignment: speaking in church!

All I had to do was read scripture one Sunday morning. I felt so nervous I had to take medication. Yet when I stood to speak, all fear disappeared. I read with ease. When I sat down, my friend, he paid me the highest compliment, "Hey, you didn't stink."

The scripture reading led to many more experiences of leading and speaking in church. By now my family had joined me in worship, and I remember our next-door neighbor saying to my mother as we walked out of church, "That son of yours is going to make a preacher someday."

Overhearing the remark, all I could think was, *Yeah . . . don't bet on it.*

But I couldn't deny that something had been lodged inside of me. Over time, I would come to understand this lodging as God's call. Many more experiences confirmed this direction: youth leadership roles, teaching opportunities, leadership in weekend spiritual retreats. Where did I find the confidence to pursue these opportunities? I know without a doubt it came from my growing understanding of the concept that sits at the foundation of faith: God loves me. How powerful to realize that you have worth in God's eyes!

I talked with my pastor to gain an understanding of what was happening to me and what I was feeling. He counseled me about what it means to be called and offered this magnificent advice: "If you pursue your call," he said, "the feeling will either grow stronger or weaker, and that is how you will know. If you can't do anything besides ordained ministry and be happy, then for God's sake, do it!"

Sitting on a pew in the empty sanctuary, we prayed that night, and I began a journey I still travel today. This call continues to take me down paths I could have never predicted. I've wished some moments could last forever as I've seen people come to faith, be renewed in faith, and experience transformation and hope. But not every step is one I've wanted to take. At times I've resented this sense of call that places its demands on me. Still I journey on, regularly asking, "God, am I on the right path? Am I going the way you want? Please, Lord, lead me."

Yes, I still struggle to know if everything I'm doing aligns with God's purpose for me. But I feel certain that God's love never fails to guide me. I also carry with me a gratitude for the Methodist church that embraced that teenage boy. Without this community, I don't know how I would have found my purpose.

I'm sharing my story so you can see how it has shaped my understanding of what it means to live with purpose. But let me state the obvious: You don't have to be a minister to have a God-given purpose! Far from it. The God I love has provided us with bountiful ways to express that divine love. God has offered us the gift of fellowship to help us in our quest for fulfillment.

What's your story, and where will it take you?

I hope this book will help you, whatever your stage in life, to discern God's leading and learn how to follow. I also hope you will use this book as part of a small-group fellowship that can encourage you along the way. A group experience also provides the opportunity to watch this study's videos, which will transport you to the actual places where Paul lived out his call.

In the chapters ahead you will explore your gifts, develop your ability to discern God's signals, respond to times when you can't live out your purpose the way you want, learn how to endure hardships and doubts, and find ways to persevere with hope and faith. Each chapter closes with a Servant Spotlight, personal testimony from an individual who—despite detours, adversity, and doubt—had the tenacity and faith to follow the guidance of a loving God.

As we begin, I invite you to pray this prayer:

Lord, help me remember that my life is a gift from you. One day I will give it back. Between now and then I want my living to matter and my days to have meaning. I believe you want me to have purpose and fulfillment, and I am open to the ways you can provide it. Show me the way, Lord. Amen.

God's love, unearned and unbound, is your starting point. Now let the journey begin.

1

PREPARING FOR PURPOSE

Having a life mission implies that the world has need of you.

—Greg Anderson

It's in Christ that we find out who we are and what we are living for.

—Ephesians 1:11, THE MESSAGE

On the evening of July 16, 1999, John Kennedy Jr.; his wife, Carolyn; and her elder sister, Lauren, took off in a private plane from a New Jersey airport. Kennedy sat in the pilot's seat, uncertified to fly with instruments and with less than an hour of experience flying at night without an instructor. Earlier, he had refused his instructor's offer to ride along because, as the instructor said, "He wanted to do it alone."

Once in the air, haze obstructed Kennedy's view of the horizon, creating a disorientation that kept him from knowing whether the plane was level or banking. He did not realize he was taking the plane into a dangerous downward spiral. It crashed just off the coast of Martha's Vineyard, Massachusetts, killing all three on board. The New York Safety Board ruled pilot error as the cause of the tragedy.[1]

Kennedy's desire to "do it alone," despite his lack of training and experience, had terrible consequences. But we understand the impulse, don't we? Self-reliance is an inherent human drive. We also live in a society that prizes individualism and independence.

This urge to "do it alone" becomes especially powerful when we seek to find our own purpose. After all, who knows better than you what direction your life should take, what you are capable of doing, and what makes you happy?

Yet research pokes holes in that notion. For instance, according to a 2013 Gallup Poll conducted globally, fewer than one in five adults worldwide described themselves as liking their daily work and being motivated to achieve their goals.[2] In 2015, according to another study, more than half of adult Americans (52.3%) reported they were *unhappy* at work—compared to 61% who in 1987, the first year the annual survey was conducted, said they liked their jobs.[3] A 2008 study concluded that four in ten adult Americans had not discovered a satisfying life purpose.[4]

We may possess the ability to do whatever we want with our lives, but it doesn't mean we can create the meaning and value we seek while doing it. We need help finding purpose. In fact, God made us that way.

RAISING A QUESTION FOR THE AGES

Our search for purpose seems coded into the fabric of our being. We are wired to live a meaningful existence, but we can't begin to discover what that purpose is unless we know the One who created us for a purpose. As Os Guinness says, "There is no calling without a caller."[5]

This quest has long vexed people of all walks of life. Among the earliest recorded search for answers is Ecclesiastes, an Old Testament book written in the ninth century BCE under the *nom de plume* "The Teacher." The entire book represents the writer's attempt to address the question, What is the meaning of life? But early on, The Teacher recognizes the futility of the quest: "None of us can ever fully understand all [God] has done, and he puts questions in our minds about the past and the future" (3:11, CEV).

It seems a cruel paradox: God has given us the desire to understand the meaning of life, but the answers lie beyond our ability to grasp. Over and over, The Teacher repeats, "Meaningless! . . . Everything is meaningless!" (1:2, NIV). Then, just about the time you think the book will end without hope, the writer concludes, "After all this, there is only one thing to say: Have reverence for God" (12:13, GNT).

Could it really be that *simple*? Perhaps, but that doesn't mean it's *simplistic*.

Every search for purpose is meant to lead us to the One who gave us the drive to search. Seeking meaning must take us to the Maker of all things. Understanding our purpose begins with knowing the One who put eternity in people's hearts.

So let's begin this journey with a straightforward proposition: We don't know ourselves completely. We need help figuring out why we are here. We need a reliable instructor. As Max Lucado says, "You cannot be anything you want to be. But you can be everything God wants you to be."[6]

USING GPS

What did we do before global positioning systems (GPS)? Honestly, I wonder now how I ever found parishioners' houses or meeting locations without it.

But despite the reliability of GPS, anyone who's used it for any length of time knows it's not totally accurate. Anything human-made has possibility for human error. Therefore, let's look to the truly perfect GPS to help us find our way: God's positioning system. As the well-known verse from Proverbs says, "Trust in the LORD with all your heart and lean not on your own understanding" (3:5, NIV).

We are not without help. God gave us a longing for purpose, but God did not leave us alone to find it. However, we have to desire the Instructor's help.

What does it look like to access divine direction? Let's return to our guide just before he started his own journey.

By the time Saul reached his early twenties, he had studied to become a Pharisee, a Jewish sect that strictly observed religious law. He counted himself among the many religious leaders in Jerusalem who advocated a zero-tolerance policy for the growing numbers of Christ-followers. They weren't called Christians at this point. The movement was simply known as The Way—perhaps a reference to the way followers found direction for living with purpose and meaning.

In his own words, Saul has an obsession with persecuting followers of the Way. (See Acts 26:11, NIV.) We can't say for sure why, though some speculate that his ambition led him to gain recognition in this manner. What we do know is that he witnessed the stoning of the first Christian martyr, Stephen (Acts 22:20), and he arrested both men and women and admitted complicity in some of their deaths (Acts 22:4).

Saul is on his way to Damascus from Jerusalem to secure more arrests when the risen Christ appears to him in a light that literally blinds him. The significance isn't lost on Saul. He has become blind to God's truth.

During the encounter, the voice of Jesus asks Saul, "Why do you persecute me? It is hard for you to kick against the goads" (Acts 26:14). What is Jesus trying to say? Adam Hamilton points out that at the time shepherds used sticks, or goads, to prod oxen or cattle.[7] In like fashion, God nudges and guides us. Resisting God's goads, Jesus says in so many words, is futile. The way to have peace comes through surrendering to and welcoming God's direction.

Now blind, Saul retreats to Damascus to fast and pray. Three days later, a Christ-follower named Ananias visits Saul to heal him. God had come to Ananias in a vision to impart this mission. With his sight restored, Saul will never see the world in the same way again. And, of course, you know the rest: Now equipped with a new faith and a calling to share grace with the world, Paul sets out to begin his work as an apostle, right?

Not so fast.

There's inconsistency between the book of Acts and Paul's own references to what happened after his conversion. Acts, which was written by the author of Luke, states that "immediately [Paul] began to proclaim" (9:20, NIV). But Paul's own account in his letter to the Galatians differs. He writes, "I went away at once into Arabia . . . then after three years I did go up to Jerusalem" (1:17-18). There he spent fifteen days with Peter, one of the twelve disciples who experienced Jesus' life and teachings firsthand. After Jerusalem, Paul returned to Tarsus for another fourteen years (2:1). Add up all this time, and Paul refers to as much as seventeen years spent in private before setting out as a missionary. ✓2↓+3

How do we account for the difference between the account in Acts and Paul's letter? These silent years may not have fit Luke's agenda. After all, his book came to be known as The Acts of the Apostles. Luke focused on the actions that took place in the early church. We don't have a definitive record of any action during the years Paul refers to in Galatians. But seventeen years is a long time. What did Paul do during this time?

Let's attempt to sketch a picture of his life during these years. I say "sketch" because Paul's letters do offer some clues about those years—years that will prepare him for his groundbreaking ministry.

STUDYING SCRIPTURE

In First Corinthians Paul writes, "I handed on to you as of first importance what I in turn had received: that Christ died for our sins in accordance with the scriptures" (15:3). Exactly when did Paul receive that information? Surely he isn't talking about his conversion experience. There's no mention of Jesus giving Paul a crucial insight. Maybe Paul receives this information in the days he spent with Peter. Maybe it comes to him in Arabia. Or maybe in Tarsus. One thing we know for sure: From this brief passage, Paul lines up this understanding of Christ with the scriptures. Considering he began at a point that justified the killing of Christians, we know he required a long time for study and reinterpretation.

What scriptures did Paul study? The New Testament did not exist at this time. In fact, Paul's letters predate the Gospels. His account of Jesus' crucifixion and resurrection are the first written proclamations of these truths. So when Paul writes about Christ dying for our sins "in accordance with the scriptures," he is talking about what we now know as the Old Testament, especially the Torah (Genesis, Exodus, Leviticus, Numbers, and Deuteronomy); the Prophets, particularly Isaiah; and historical books like Kings and Chronicles.

As a learned Pharisee, Paul could have recited large amounts of scripture from memory. But his experience with Christ forces Paul to interpret these familiar passages in a new light. He feels compelled to align his new revelation of God's presence in the world with the old revelation that has always informed his living. Returning to the scriptures he knew so well, he now finds compelling prophetic evidence not only of the coming of Jesus Christ but also of Christ's mission in the world.

Paul doesn't throw scripture out the window. Instead, he seeks to bring all he has known into accordance with all he has just learned from his conversion experience.

STICKING TO HIS KNITTING

Paul does more than figure out his new faith. The book of Acts says he begins preaching in the synagogues and "proving that Jesus was the Messiah" (9:22). The word *prove* in Greek means "to knit together." Even as Paul preaches in the synagogue, he knits together his new understanding of scripture and his experience with Christ.

Is not proof — texting

When we talk about someone preaching today, we picture a person standing before a congregation and using a one-way form of communication. But given the meaning of the Greek word, could preaching have looked different in Paul's day?

My own observations from travels in Greece make me wonder. On a recent trip I saw people gathering at sidewalk cafés, especially men. Our guide explained the importance of this practice to the culture. These public places provide forums for people to meet and discuss issues and politics. Instead of allowing the media to be the sole influence, they hash out significant matters through dialogue.

Could this represent what preaching was like for Paul? Maybe the synagogue offers a time and place for discussion and debate. Perhaps he uses these gatherings as opportunities to present his reasoning on how Jesus can be the Messiah and what that means about the nature and character of God.

In the church I serve, the word *connect* holds great significance. The church staff and members stress the importance not only of coming to worship but also of joining small groups and classes. Typically these groups study and reflect on the same passages of scripture. The insights I hear in groups I'm part of always amaze me. People often share reflections and wisdom about scripture that give me a new understanding and appreciation (not to mention occasional envy that someone sees something I didn't).

Christian faith in the New Testament is understood in the context of community. If we choose to live our lives in isolation, our skills and talents are unavailable to others and the qualities we lack remain outside our reach.

LISTENING AND PRAYER

Paul refers to "revelation" several times in his letters. For example, he writes this to the Galatians: "I want you to know, brothers and sisters, that the gospel that was proclaimed by me is not of human origin; for I did not receive it from a human source, nor was I taught it, but I received it through a revelation of Jesus Christ" (1:11-12). In his letter to the Ephesians he speaks of "how the mystery was made known to me by revelation" (3:3).

I believe these revelations come because Paul takes the time to develop a personal, living relationship with Jesus Christ. Surely Paul had never had a spiritual experience like the one he had on the Damascus road. He must have spent the following years learning to listen and live in communion with God through Jesus Christ.

When I traveled to Tarsus to film the video companion to this book, I got to spend an afternoon by the quiet pools and waterfalls of the Cydnus River. I imagined Paul spending hours there alone, sitting on a rock or by a secluded riverbank praying and listening to

God. This time clearly had a huge impact on his life as an apostle. As we will see in the pages ahead, God interrupts Paul many times—sometimes to redirect him, other times to give assurance. That ability to recognize God's voice results from Paul's investment of time in the years between conversion and calling.

ESPOUSING A CHANGED WORLDVIEW

Last of all, Paul probably spends this time transforming his worldview. Before the Damascus road, Paul had a clear and simple purpose: Tell people how to live and let them know where they're falling short. Paul's experience with Christ changes his understanding of God's nature. He shifts from telling people how to live to understanding what they need.

As Paul writes to the Ephesians, "Although I am the very least of all the saints, this grace was given to me to bring to the Gentiles the news of the boundless riches of Christ, and to make everyone see what is the plan of the mystery hidden for ages in God who created all things. . . . This was in accordance with the eternal purpose that he has carried out in Christ Jesus our Lord" (3:8-9, 11). Paul takes seventeen years to put all of this together. In that time he reinterprets scripture, prays, listens to God, and meditates on the meaning of his revelations for God's larger purpose in creation.

So what does this mean for us? How do we emulate Paul's steps to discover our purpose for living?

First of all, let's understand that when we spend time as Paul did—praying, meditating, studying, talking, listening, growing—we aren't unlocking the mystery to our purpose. We are already living out our purpose! God made us for relationship with God and one another and to revel in the life God has given us. As Paul wrote in his second letter to Timothy, "[God] saved us and called us with a holy calling, not according to our works but according to [God's] own purpose and grace" (1:9).

Starting with God

Paul begins living out his purpose when he stops trying to gain God's favor and simply embraces the fact that he is already favored. He finds out the hard way that trying to earn God's blessing can lead to things not of God's blessing. But at least he discovers it! As theologian Paul Tillich wrote, "Man must accept that he is accepted; he must accept acceptance."[8]

Living with purpose means living with the constant affirmation that we belong to God and are meant to enjoy God's company. Paul writes to the Ephesians: "It's in Christ that we find out who we are and what we are living for" (1:11, The Message). We exist to pursue a relationship with God in the company of a spiritual family that helps us experience God's presence and hear God's voice.

Living out a purpose of knowing God means we also desire what God desires. What does God want? The Bible makes that clear in its continuous story of God's determination to liberate people—from themselves and the power of sin; from conditions of injustice and poverty; and from others who enslave, oppress, and exploit.

God relies on us to hasten this vision of God's reign and find our place in the grander scheme of eternity.

Living out a purpose of knowing God also means giving ourselves away. Jesus' words inspire our calling: "The Son of Man did not come to be served, but to serve, and to give his life as a ransom for many" (Mark 10:45, NIV). In that sacrifice, we also receive the promise of new life, just as Jesus assures with these words: "Unless a kernel of wheat falls to the ground and dies, it remains only a single seed. But if it dies, it produces many seeds" (John 12:24, NIV).

The must die to ourselves - what is this? How?

What does God Need?

Ok that's what we came to do - we are not that

God's purpose for us is awesome—and greater than any particular expression of that purpose. What does that mean? It means our own purpose should be adaptable to whatever station or stage we find ourselves in life. Think about it: If we define our purpose as our career, what happens when we retire? If we define our purpose as raising a family, what happens when our children grow up and leave home? The fact is, true purpose refuses to be compartmentalized. Following God's direction means being available to the ways God can use us at any moment in our lives . . . which takes us back to Paul.

What Paul does during those seventeen years isn't a matter of downloading coordinates on where to go in life. Instead, he tunes his receiver and boosts his amplifier. He spends time learning how to live in constant communion with Christ.

If we desire to live in harmony with God and to be open to the ways God can use us, then how and where we express our purpose will change many times. In the chapters ahead we will explore what it means to face the changes and challenges of following God's direction. For now, let's continue this journey with the most critical step in the process: identifying our reason for living.

CRAFTING A PERSONAL MISSION STATEMENT

Why comes before *what*. Understanding *why* you're here helps define *what* you do. *often the why is discovered thru the what*

Jack Groppel, cofounder of the Johnson & Johnson Human Performance Institute, an Orlando-based coaching firm, encourages clients to identify their *why* through a personal life-mission statement. He points to the frequent failure of keeping New Year's resolutions as an example of the need to have a defined *why* in life.

"A resolution is a well-intended action plan," Groppel says, "but because a person hasn't really connected to the 'why' behind it, the old way of life, the chaos, comes back into play and they can't really sustain it."[9] *Why we must "die"*

Knowing our *why* helps us focus on doing the important *whats*. How do you go about crafting a personal mission statement? Here are some guidelines to help you:

- Make sure it is in keeping with the purposes of God and the character of Christ. Before God calls you to *do*, God calls you to *be*. Who do you believe God calls you to be?

- Make it about more than you. A purpose that focuses only on your happiness or success, no matter how altruistic, can set you up for disappointment. What positive impact can you make and bring to others?

- Don't limit your purpose to a specific role or location. Can you carry out your purpose until the day you die?

With that in mind, let's take a look at some popular mission statements. The condensed version of Jesus' personal mission statement is Luke 19:10, "The Son of Man came to seek and save the lost" (NIV). Earlier in the same Gospel, Jesus expands on this notion using the words of Isaiah: "The Spirit of the Lord is on me, because he has anointed me to proclaim good news to the poor. He has sent me to proclaim freedom for the prisoners and recovery of sight for the blind, to set the oppressed free, to proclaim the year of the Lord's favor" (Luke 4:18-19, NIV).

Paul states his personal mission in this way: "God has appointed me as an apostle and teacher to proclaim the Good News" (2 Tim. 1:11, GNT).

Clearly all these statements are in keeping with the purposes of God and not limited to specific jobs or places. And obviously, both Jesus and Paul lived out these mission statements to their deaths.

The personal mission statement of my episcopal leader in Indiana, Bishop Julius C. Trimble, is "to encourage all people with the love of Jesus Christ to rise to their highest potential."[10]

My personal mission statement is "to honor God and help others find and give hope through Jesus Christ."

So now it's time to work on your statement. Start by thinking about specific words that describe how you seek to live out your relationship with God. Write them down in a list. Read through the list, and see which ones resonate with a yes! Now consider how your life can reflect the values of God. What does God want to do through you? What reflects your own passions, interests, and abilities?

As you work to form a statement, keep it simple and direct. These words are meant to guide and inspire you, not to specify all the ways you may live out your purpose.

It's also crucial to resist reducing your statement to something you have always lived up to. When I placed "to honor God" in my statement, I acknowledged it as far more of a challenge than a reflection of reality—because I often fall short. Some days I have to ask myself if I am honoring God with a slumped spirit and defeated attitude. Other times I question whether I am honoring God in the way I treat people. I may not always get it right, but when I recognize my faults, I seek to make amends and get back on track with my mission.

CONSIDERING THE END OF IT ALL

We aren't told how Paul died, though we know he was imprisoned in Rome, and tradition says he was beheaded there. Imagine a conversation with Paul in those last days:

Paul, how did you get here?
By boat.
No, I mean, why are you here?

Because I was faithful to the end.

Faithful to what?

Doing what the Lord Jesus Christ called me to do, to share the good news of his grace. I believe what I did was worth it. You see, I know firsthand the misery of the human heart when we either don't care about pleasing God or we believe we can never do enough to please God. When I started from the point that I already please God, I became a different person—a person who sought to give life and hope. That is what Jesus Christ did for me, and I saw the difference he made to thousands of people as I invited them to accept Christ. That's why I'm here.

I can imagine Paul saying something like that. And then I can imagine him asking me: Now why are you here?

SERVANT SPOTLIGHT

Eric Howard Tells His Story

In 1994 I found myself full of what this world had to offer yet constantly parched, empty, longing—knowing life held something more. I grew up with a nominal faith, having never heard the gospel message. In July 6, 1994, in a hotel room in Bloomsburg, Pennsylvania, I let Christ in. That one event forever altered the trajectory of my life, what for me redefined purpose and flipped my world upside down. That one moment is seared into my heart. Christ captured my heart.

I walked outside the room down the hall and through the bar. On my way outside a man stopped me, an acquaintance of sorts, and he asked if I would like to talk about what had just occurred. I was floored. How did this person know I had just had a powerful spiritual experience? We walked around the town as he shared what it means to be a follower of Christ. We spoke about freedom, challenge, and a battle that would last for the rest of my life. We spoke of change, dying to self, and what it means to feed the soul.

Over the next twelve months I made important decisions, separating from unhealthy influences that had entrenched me in sin and defrauded me emotionally, while at the same time seeking forgiveness from individuals I had hurt and taken advantage of. I started changing behaviors and developed a relationship with Christ. During this time I discovered Micah 6:8— an amazing verse that calls us to act justly, love mercy, and walk humbly with God. That verse flipped the script in my world.

During this period of time I read a report about homeless teens in Indianapolis. Something inside me wanted to leap into action. If Christ could change me, Christ could extend hope to anyone. I was told I lacked the background and education to start serving the homeless. I was told it was too dangerous. With what I perceived as overwhelming odds and armed with nothing more than peanut butter and jelly sandwiches, I got started. I met kids on the street and offered them something to eat. Overwhelmed and tired, questioning if I had heard *God's* call correctly, I received an anonymous note one day, "Eric, God sometimes calls the qualified but always qualifies the called." That affirmation kept me from bailing on this mission to help homeless teenagers.

Twenty years later, the ministry of Outreach, Inc., is still going strong and seeking to love homeless young people in the Indianapolis community authentically. Many religious communities and organizations support our work now. We are changing a generation one life at a time. There's nothing like hearing a homeless young person say, "I'm alive because of Outreach." All we do is show love. We talk and listen to kids. We visit them in the hospitals and jails. When they are selling their bodies or struggling with addictions, we see the persons behind the problems. It all started in a hotel room where God found me, gave me hope, and said, "I have a job for you to do."

REFLECTION QUESTIONS

- Do you currently have a purpose? Can you state it aloud? What is its source?

- What does your purpose or lack thereof say about the meaning of life?

- How do you currently seek God's guidance for your life?

- Who do you believe God calls you to be?

- What positive impact can you make and bring to others?

- What would it look like for you to take God's call on your life and your ability to make a positive impact and combine them into a lifelong purpose?

2

TAKING STOCK

The truth is not that God is finding us a place for our gifts but that God has created us and our gifts for a place of [God's] choosing— and we will only be ourselves when we are finally there.

—Os Guinness

Isn't everything you have and everything you are sheer gifts from God?

—1 Corinthians 4:7, THE MESSAGE

When my wife's family gets together for Christmas in Kansas, we spend our days relaxing, watching sports, worshiping together, and most of all—eating. In fact, we snack our way through the holidays. In celebration of this time-honored tradition, one year my sisters-in-law created a version of the Food Network's cooking-competition show *Iron Chef* as an all-family activity. One sister-in-law is a pastor so we were able to use the large kitchen at her church.

Following the rules of the game, we formed two teams; each team took turns picking ingredients that awaited us in the kitchen. Once one team picked an ingredient, it was off limits to the other team. We quickly realized this rule meant we could play both offense and defense. When one team picked spaghetti noodles, for instance, the other selected the tomato sauce. There went that Italian menu! After one team picked taco meat, the other team grabbed up the tortillas. So much for a traditional Mexican dish. You see how it went. This family is a very competitive bunch.

By the end of the selection process, both teams were left with a hodgepodge of foods that wouldn't show up on any recipe's ingredient list. And yet we had to cook. Even worse, we had to eat it—because not only was this a competition, but this would also be our dinner.

Fortunately, a few creative cooks in the family were ready to improvise. (I was put to work chopping onions. Thanks, guys.) Miraculously, an hour later we all sat down to two full (and, surprisingly, tasty) meals. The judging was fierce, and, yes, I am still nursing a grudge that the taco spaghetti edged out my team's veggie enchiladas.

If your life were made into a cooking competition, what would it be like: an *Iron Chef*-style challenge or a chili cook-off? They are two different kinds of contests. One compels you to cook with the ingredients on hand. The other is based on recipes.

Some people try to write their life stories this way. They come up with what they think will be a winning "main course"—CEO of a company, medical specialist, attorney, politician—and start gathering the ingredients needed to get there. The problem comes when the ingredients—the abilities and traits required—don't necessarily line up with who they are.

A member of my church experienced this "ingredient disparity." He graduated from a small liberal arts college with a degree in economics and took an executive position with a pharmaceutical company. He was on his way to a lucrative career, except for one thing. His passions lay elsewhere. A standout college athlete, he really wanted to coach basketball. One day he decided to follow his heart and pitched himself to the coaching staff of Butler University in Indianapolis. They offered him an unpaid position to review game film, and he quit his job to take it. Crazy, right? Yet a year later Butler promoted him to full-time assistant coach. Six years later, he became head coach, eventually taking Butler to two consecutive national championship games. Today Brad Stevens is head coach of the Boston Celtics of the NBA.[1]

How different life looks when we begin with the ingredients we have on hand rather than with a standard recipe.

STRANGE INGREDIENTS FOR AN APOSTLE?

At first glance it would be tempting to say Paul doesn't fit the ideal recipe for an apostle. As a proud Pharisee, he not only reveres the traditions of his faith but also antagonizes Christ-followers. He is well educated while many of the leaders of the early church are illiterate. Yet God uses everything about Paul's life to carry out a purpose of sharing with the world the message of hope through Jesus Christ.

In the following chapter I will sketch out a profile of Paul by looking at key elements of his life: cultural background, spiritual upbringing, personal life, education and skills, and experiences. As I do, I'll ask you to take a moment to pause and reflect on what those elements look like in your own life. Then you'll begin sketching out your own profile and putting together a spiritual inventory to help you understand your God-given gifts, passions, and style. (Visit Rob-Fuquay.com for guidance.) Combined, these will give you a better idea of who you are. With this starting point, you will uncover clues to solving the mystery of God's direction for your life.

Let's begin with Paul's cultural background and the place where he grew up, Tarsus of Cilicia, which he once called "no ordinary city" (Acts 21:39). Two main features give Tarsus this reputation: its commercial importance and its significance as a university city. Located along strategic east-west trade routes just twelve miles inland from the Mediterranean Sea, Tarsus was a melting pot of cultures, religions, and languages. In Paul's day, Tarsus played a significant role in the Roman Empire, giving it political influence. Its educational opportunities rivaled those in Athens and Alexandria.

Paul grew up in a culture with significant Greek influence, beginning four centuries before when Alexander the Great marched into Tarsus on his campaign eastward, leaving his mark in his wake. In Paul's day, Greek philosophers stood on street corners practicing their rhetoric and seeking to persuade listeners. Again, how might these experiences have influenced young Paul?

Now pause. What about you? Where did you grow up? Was it an urban or a rural setting? Were you reared in the same place, or did you move a lot? What influences stand out as you think about the dominant culture of your upbringing? Did you experience racial, ethnic, and cultural diversity? Were their prejudices in the community? What did your culture value? How much did geography play a part? Put all that together, and what would you say are the two or three most influential aspects of your cultural background that have shaped who you are today?

Next, let's think about Paul's spiritual upbringing. He was reared in a conservative Jewish home, acutely aware of his religious heritage. The name he used through the initial portion of his life, Saul, strongly reflected his Jewish identity and was perhaps inspired by the first king of Israel. His Greek name, Paul, reflects another aspect of his family identity.

When Paul wrote to the Philippians he mentioned this strong religious influence: "Circumcised on the eighth day, a member . . .

of the tribe of Benjamin" (Phil. 3:5). By mentioning his circumcision, Paul communicated his family's adherence to the requirements of Jewish laws. In Tarsus, Jewish residents were most likely Diaspora Jews, meaning they had descended from families who fled Israel during times of persecution in previous centuries. So far removed from the more orthodox environment of Israelite communities, many identified themselves as Jewish by faith rather than practice, at least in terms of strict adherence to all details of religious laws. By mentioning his circumcision Paul signals his family's devotion.

Again, consider your upbringing. What faith influence did you experience in your home? Did faith play a significant role? Did you worship regularly, observe religious holidays, and practice rituals like prayers before meals and at bedtime? Or was faith understood but not practiced?

If you didn't have a strong faith influence, this assessment isn't intended as judgment. Just honestly appraise your spiritual upbringing and consider how God would view it. If you had little or no faith influence, how may God use your background to help you relate to people who share that upbringing?

The passage in Philippians also notes Paul's Jewish tribal heritage. He grew up knowing his lineage. That childhood knowledge is as valuable now as it was back then—a view that recent research supports. Two Emory University psychologists, Marshall Duke and Robyn Fivush, have devised a measure called the "Do You Know?" scale that asks children twenty questions about their family history, such as "Do you know where your grandparents grew up?" and "Do you know where your parents met?" After extensive interviews with children, the researchers came to a fascinating conclusion: The more the young subjects knew about their families, the more self-esteem they had. Indeed, Duke and Fivush discovered their "Do You Know?" scale was "the single predictor of children's emotional health and happiness."[2]

Think about your own family's background. How much do you know? How far can you trace your genealogy? What key turning points occurred in your family history, such as an immigration, a financial windfall, a premature death? Perhaps a historic event, such as famine or war, caused a major transition.

Next, let's look at Paul's personal life, though the information is scarce. As far as we know Paul never married. We can assume he grew up with both parents; otherwise, scripture mentions only a sister and a nephew (Acts 23:16). In fact, Paul may have lived with his sister's family when he went to Jerusalem at a young age to study under Gamaliel, a respected Jewish law teacher in the city (Acts 5:34). If that's the case, then we know that adults besides Paul's parents strongly influenced his personal life.

Many adults influenced me as a child, including one I only recently learned about from my dad. One night he and I were discussing *The Help*, the novel (and subsequent film) about a group of African American maids who served several white families in Jackson, Mississippi. "You know, that was my story," my dad said. He went on to fill in gaps of his life that I'd never heard.

He grew up in the 1930s and '40s in Durham, North Carolina, and his father abandoned the family when my dad was two. To support her two sons, my grandmother took a job at a local tobacco factory. She made enough money to afford "help," a black woman named Lily. My dad said she was like a mother to him. "She raised me and I loved her dearly," he told me.

For years, I had wondered why I'd emerged from my childhood in North Carolina without some of the prejudices so prevalent in the culture around me. Now I finally knew. I had a whole new appreciation and gratitude for a woman I had never met, a woman who helped shape my life.

In your family circle, who exerted the most influence in your young life? What relatives or surrogate family members made the most difference in shaping your life?

Next let's consider Paul's education and skills. As we've already observed, Paul was reared in a community that valued education. Not only that, he moved to Jerusalem at a young age to study under Gamaliel. We read of this teacher's enormous influence in the early days of the church when members of the Sanhedrin, the ruling religious council, were ready to round up and execute all the apostles. Gamaliel's level-headed response changed the mood of the council: "Keep away from these men and let them alone because if this plan or this undertaking is of human origin, it will fail; but if it is of God, you will not be able to overthrow them—in that case you may even be found fighting against God!" (Acts 5:38-39). Gamaliel's words exemplify the proverb: "A soft answer turns away wrath" (Prov. 15:1).

So who were the mentors—teachers, coaches, scout leaders, counselors—who most influenced you? Which teachers instilled a passion to learn and made you feel gifted and capable?

In addition to his education, Paul also learned a trade: tent-making, which paid off later in life. Tarsus was known for its production of a durable material made from goats' skin ideally suited for tents. Paul employed this trade while he lived in Corinth (Acts 18:3) and probably in other places, as well.

What gifts, talents, and skills do you have? Do you have natural abilities that have distinguished you? Academic, artistic, athletic, analytical, interpersonal? Which of these natural abilities have you cultivated? Which have you not fully explored?

The idea of natural abilities is worth examining further. Some people feel these abilities are "God-given" and exist for use in explicitly religious purposes. William Wilberforce, a member of British Parliament in the eighteenth century, dedicated his life to abolishing the slave trade. But he nearly missed that calling. When he came to faith, he connected his conversion experience to his passion for reform, and he felt that meant he needed to leave politics and enter the ministry. The counsel of John Newton, the reformed slave ship captain who wrote the hymn "Amazing Grace," changed his mind. Newton challenged Wilberforce to see his role in politics as a calling and said, "It's hoped and believed that the Lord has raised you up for the good of the nation."[3] Wilberforce heeded this advice and spent the rest of his life fighting for the oppressed.

I think about Paul working as a tent maker and using his vocation to further his call. I picture him plying his trade as a way to get to know other business owners and customers, using these opportunities to build relationships and share his faith in Christ. In other words, Paul brought his passion for sharing faith in Christ to his work.

Not long ago I was in Talladega, Alabama, and went to a Mexican restaurant for dinner. A young waiter came to the table and started pouring water. I thanked him and then he shocked me with these words: "It's my blessing to serve you." Not exactly the kind of thing you expect a young man to say while filling a water glass.

"I appreciate the blessing language," I told him, and he responded, "Well, that's just what I do. I love telling people about God's love."

I struck up a conversation, and he told me he was working his way through college and had hopes of attending seminary one day. He said he felt called to ministry, but he wasn't waiting until he received a degree to begin. He wasn't simply doing a job; he was living out his purpose.

How does God see your livelihood as an opportunity to fulfill your purpose? Where do you spend most of your waking hours? Taking care of your family? Working in a store? Sitting behind a desk? Answering a phone? Doing shift work in a factory? What if your co-workers, associates, or clients are not just folks related to your job but also are the people with whom you can live out your purpose? What would that look like?

Now before I finish sketching out Paul, let's think about one more aspect of his life: his experiences. God used these elements of Paul's life also. We don't know many formative experiences in his life—childhood events or unrecorded episodes during his ministry. But some experiences we do know, not all of which were flattering. Paul had blood on his hands. He participated in the stoning death of the apostle Stephen, which meant he lived out his days burdened by that memory.

We know of times when Paul lost his temper. We also know of painful experiences: nearly stoned to death, floggings, shipwreck, near death from snake bite. He spent years in prison cells; faced riots, angry mobs, and false accusations. He was slapped and spat on. But in his opinion, nothing lay beyond God's ability to use: "[God] consoles us in all our affliction, so that we may be able to console those who are in any affliction with the consolation with which we ourselves are consoled by God" (2 Cor. 1:4). Paul understood that God doesn't waste tears.

A retired couple who recently joined the church I pastor shared with me the greatest pain of their lives. Some years ago, they lost their adult son to cancer, a tragedy, the father said, that became an obstacle in their relationship with God. But I knew that obstacle had been cleared when the father asked me about volunteering with Stephen Ministry to help other parents who experience the death of a child.

What tears have you shed in your life? What are your heartaches and disappointments? What failures and regrets do you have? We will say more in chapter 5 about God's power to use failure, but for now think of these experiences as realities that make up who you are. In God's hands such realities become redemptive.

THE FACTS OF YOUR LIFE

Have you answered all the questions for your personal profile? Take a look at the questions on page 48. How many have you reflected on and answered for yourself? These facts of your life are the ingredients you bring to the search for how God may use you. When detectives attempt to solve a mystery, they spread out all the known facts of the case: pictures, evidence, witness statements. These clues help them get at the truth.

If you are in the dark about knowing God's direction for your life, start with your profile. See what is before you that, when assembled, can offer some insight. Then ask God, "What would you like to do with this?"

Once you've completed your profile, it's time to work on an inventory. Many great tools are available to help you assess the dimensions of your life (see page 51), but any popular inventory generally includes at least three features that can be remembered with the acronym I introduced in chapter 1: GPS. This time the letters stand for Gifts, Passions, and Style. (Go to RobFuquay.com for directions.)

Gifts represent the traits and abilities God places in people to benefit others. Paul has much to say on this topic in both Romans 12 and in 1 Corinthians 12. Paul teaches that healthy churches assign tasks according to people's gifts.

You have unique gifts. This is the way God made you. You realize you are living out of your gifts when tasks that employ these natural abilities give you energy rather than drain you. As the saying goes, "Do what you love to do, and you'll never work a day in your life."

Passions involve what stirs your soul. You can identify your passions in several ways, but one tried-and-true method is to ask, "What topic or interest could you stay up all night talking about?" Another insight into passion is to consider what lights your fuse. What problem or ill in our world fires you up and makes you say, "This cannot continue!"

As a parent it's fun to watch your kids discover their passions. The oldest of my three daughters feels especially passionate about animal rights and the environment. Accept an invitation from her to watch a documentary on the unethical treatment of animals or the disappearing rainforests, and you can count on a discussion afterward that will go for hours. Often she can't talk about these topics without tearing up. Seeing her gifts and passions align is exciting to watch.

Finally, *Style* is the way we work and accomplish tasks, which can either help or hinder our ability to work with joy. Do you like working alone or on a team? Do you enjoy dreaming up the projects or following clear directions? Do you like working with people or doing physical tasks?

The above offer some ways of understanding the environment in which we use our gifts and pursue our passions. They can make all the difference in our effectiveness and sense of fulfillment.

A Servant's Heart

Before closing this chapter, I shall mention one more quality essential to living with purpose: the attitude in which we live. Again, let's remember this book's perspective. This is not a career-finder resource or a way to figure out how to be happy. This book is intended to launch a discussion of understanding your purpose from the foundational belief that you are a child of God.

You were born with a unique combination of talents and personality that factor into the ways God can use you to carry out God's purpose. This is the key to understanding our purpose in life: understanding how our story fits into God's bigger purposes for this world.

Therefore I would be remiss not to give attention to the one character flaw that can throw a monkey wrench in this whole process. We can know our profile and inventory. We can find useful places for God to put us to work. We can even feel a sense of reward in making a difference in others' lives. But without a servant's heart, our actions will be self-serving.

The magnetic pull of the human personality is to look out for number one. This pull can show up anywhere, even when it comes to letting our lives be used purposefully. Our attempts to be compassionate, generous, and other-focused can turn into what makes us feel important, recognized, and rewarded. Yet, the aim of the Christian life is to "let the same mind be in you that was in Christ Jesus" (Phil. 2:5).

Think for just a moment about the purpose of Jesus' life. Invoking the words of Isaiah, Jesus identified his mission: "The Spirit of the Lord is on me, because he has anointed me to proclaim good news to the poor. He has sent me to proclaim freedom for the prisoners and recovery of sight for the blind, to set the oppressed free, to proclaim the year of the Lord's favor" (Luke 4:18-19, NIV).

It is worth taking time to ponder those words and how Jesus fulfilled them in his life. But think of other statements Jesus made that identified his mission. He came to rescue people from sin (Matt. 1:23), from emptiness (John 10:10), from being lost (Luke 19:10), and from death (John 3:16). In total, Jesus' life purpose was to bring hope to the world. *- "that you might have "Life in all its fulness"*

But consider too how Jesus fulfilled that mission: He willingly gave his life for others (John 10:18). God's way of bringing hope comes through self-giving, sacrificial love. Jesus also once told his followers that "the Son of Man came not to be served but to serve, and to give his life a ransom for many" (Matt. 20:28). As important as what Jesus did was how he did it. He set the example for his followers. So if we are to apply our Christian faith to this business of living with purpose, then it will involve our willingness to serve. In other words, God's direction is not so much about the places we go as the people we become.

Cuban-born TV host Daisy Fuentes tells a moving account of how she got involved in the work of St. Jude Children's Research Hospital in Memphis, Tennessee.[4] A devout Catholic and a person of deep faith, Daisy was introduced to the hospital's work by actress Marlo Thomas, daughter of St. Jude's founder, the late actor and comedian Danny Thomas. At first Marlo simply asked Daisy to appear at a fund-raiser in Los Angeles, which was easy enough for someone comfortable in front of crowds. But then, Daisy recalled in an article she wrote for *Guideposts* magazine, Marlo made her uncomfortable with the next invitation: "Come to the hospital and meet the kids."

Daisy struggled with this request. She knew most of the children were desperately ill with cancer and wondered how she could ever help, but Marlo's words struck deep: "Just being with them makes a big difference." Daisy remembered a period in her life just as her career was taking off when her mother, the "glue" of her family, found out she had breast cancer. Her mother was the one who kept everyone else steady, and now she needed support.

Through this experience with her mom, Daisy discovered the primary way to help someone in sickness. "I couldn't make her well. I couldn't take her fear away, but I could sit with her in the radiology waiting room. I didn't even have to say anything. It was enough for her to know she wasn't alone."

Daisy recalled this experience as she reflected on the opportunity to be healing and helpful to children in crisis. She went to St. Jude's. During the visit, an encounter with a nine-year-old girl named Jessica especially touched her. Seriously ill with leukemia, "she didn't let any of that get in the way of her bubbly personality," Daisy wrote. "I hugged her goodbye knowing that I might never see her again, the odds seemed so stacked against her."

But years later, Jessica, now healthy and doing well, wrote to tell Daisy how significant her attention was in helping her face her illness.

We never know how God will use our experiences, position, and personality to give us direction. But our gifts don't mean anything if we don't make them available.

A servant's heart may be the door God uses to to shift you in a new direction.

Are you ready to answer God's knock?

SERVANT SPOTLIGHT
Reverend Charles Harrison Tells His Story

God has used the events of my life to put me in places I could have never imagined over thirty years ago. I grew up in Jeffersonville, Indiana, a small town just across the Ohio River from Louisville, Kentucky. My stepbrother lived in a high-crime, drug-infested area on the west side of Louisville. I spent a lot of time with him. In his late teens his involvement in criminal activities made him a victim of the streets.

I was fourteen when I learned my brother had been shot and killed by a gang. Rage seized me. I had a good idea who was responsible and felt determined to take revenge. I obtained a gun and was planning my strategy to take down my brother's killers until men in my church blocked my path—literally.

The men had gotten wind of my plan. They tracked me down and said, "Charles, we are not going to let you do this." They surrounded me and held me as I collapsed in their arms sobbing. They helped me redirect my anger and focus on being the man God wanted me to be. I discovered how much God believes in me because of these men who believed in what I could become.

Some years later I responded to a call to ministry and went to college and seminary. After serving seven years in a black congregation in New Castle, I was appointed to a black urban congregation in Indianapolis. This congregation was located at ground zero for violence in the city. Burdened by the fear that engulfed my congregation, I attended an event that featured two pastors who were members of the Boston Ten Point Coalition. They talked about the role the church played in helping reduce youth violence in that city. A group of volunteers routinely walk the streets in the roughest neighborhoods of the city. They establish relationships with at-risk youth on the streets to redirect their lives and put them on a path of success.

A few days later I met with several pastors in the city of Indianapolis, and that day we formed the Indianapolis Ten Point Coalition. Every Friday and Saturday nights we walk the streets getting to know families, learning the names of the children, finding out what is happening in their lives, and doing what we can to prevent crime and violence. Hundreds of volunteers, many of them ex-cons, have joined this effort. We have seen incredible success in the neighborhoods where Ten Point has a presence. When potential trouble arises, we make sure we have one another's backs. Twenty years later we still have a strong presence on the streets.

Occasionally I travel to other cities and talk about the work we are doing in Indianapolis. I often wonder how a poor kid from Jeffersonville got here, but then I realize nothing in our lives is off limits to God. When we let God use everything about us, the good and bad, there is no telling where God will take us.

REFLECTION QUESTIONS

The Hunt

- What are the two or three most influential aspects of your cultural background that have shaped who you are today?

Edna

- What sort of faith influence was in your home, if any?
- Who had the most influence in your young life? In what ways?
- Who were the mentors who most influenced you? How?
- What gifts, talents, and skills do you have? Which remain unexplored?
- How does God see your livelihood as an opportunity to fulfill your purpose?
- What failures, regrets, heartaches, or disappointments do you have? What do they say about your purpose?

The following are among the popular life inventories offered by Christian sources:

- Saddleback Church, actually a cluster of campuses in Southern California, uses an assessment program called S.H.A.P.E., which stands for Spiritual Gifts, Heart (passion), Abilities, Personality, and Experiences. Pastor Rick Warren and his team offer classes and curriculum that help participants identify their gifts and goals, as well as "how to have the most fulfilling life possible."

- A number of churches use the S.T.R.I.D.E. assessment as part of its Spiritual Gifts Discovery program. Featured in Carol Cartmill and Yvonne Gentile's study, *Serving from the Heart: Finding Your Gifts and Talents for Service* (Abingdon Press, 2011), S.T.R.I.D.E. stands for Spiritual gifts, Talents, Resources, Individuality, Dreams, and Experiences.

- Max Lucado, the author and pastor of Oak Hills Church in San Antonio, Texas, relies on S.T.O.R.Y., an assessment survey featured in Lucado's book *Cure for the Common Life* (Thomas Nelson, 2008). S.T.O.R.Y. stands for Strengths, Topic (interests), Optimal Conditions, Relationships, and "Yes!" moments (passion).

3

FACING ADVERSITY

"The Christian ideal has not been tried and found wanting. It has been found difficult; and left untried."

—G. K. Chesterton

At the end of our lives, it's the troubles we faced for the sake of a greater cause that will have the greatest meaning.

—John Ortberg

Have you ever tried to help someone only to have your efforts rewarded with a slap on the back . . . of your head? My most memorable Sunday school lesson occurred in high school. My teacher challenged the class to do some kind of "secret" service. The directions were simple: Identify a task that would help someone; then do it, and don't tell anyone. The point was to learn humility by performing a good deed without receiving recognition. *Mt 6:1-4*

Didn't follow thru

Later that week I saw my chance while out driving. I spotted a mailbox almost hidden by overgrown weeds. I knew a lot of elderly residents lived in this neighborhood, so I assumed whoever lived in this house was too frail to keep up with these sorts of chores. (Of course, you know the old saying about what happens when you assume. I was well on my way.) I hurried home to fetch some yard tools and soon was out clearing away the weeds.

Then, just in the middle of my good deed, a car pulled into the driveway, and a healthy-looking middle-aged man got out.

"What are you doing on my property?" he asked.

The accusatory tone shocked me. "I'm just trying to be helpful," I stammered.

"I didn't ask you to do that," he said. "Why are you doing it?"

Now, the jig was up. I told him the whole story: the Sunday school lesson, my good intentions, my wrong assumptions. I figured he would say, "Okay then, finish up."

Instead, he said, "That's the dumbest thing I ever heard. Now get off my property!"

I stood there dumbfounded as he got back in his car and headed up the driveway. Then I loaded up my tools and turned toward home, thinking maybe he was right. This was the dumbest Sunday school lesson in the history of Christian education!

The next Sunday our teacher asked us to share any learnings from our efforts. One after another, my classmates talked about the warm, gooey feelings they'd experienced from secretly helping someone else. Then my turn arrived and, haltingly, I shared my story.

"Frankly," I told my classmates, "doing this embarrassed me. It felt lousy."

Fortunately, my Sunday school teacher was a person of great grace. My feelings, he told me, were understandable. He was sorry the man didn't value my intentions. But then he continued, "Could it have been that your service was more about your need than the man's?

And while you may not have done it for recognition, did you have an expectation about the way your service should make you feel?"

My teacher went on to suggest that the task could have presented an even deeper lesson for me than humility. "Sometimes," he said, "trying to help people can create conflict for ourselves."

Sometimes trying to help people can create conflict for ourselves. At the time those words didn't make much sense. But they've grown to mean a lot over the years. Surely anyone who has engaged in deeds of compassion and service to others knows it doesn't always turn out rosy. This is the underbelly of living out God's purpose for our lives. It can be hard as heck!

A lifetime of ministry has certainly shown me this is true, and nowhere is it more evident than in the church. As the late Joan Rivers said, "Can we talk?" Over the years, I've watched newcomers join a congregation, thinking it's immune to political arguments, knee-jerk judgments, lingering resentments, hurt feelings. Sooner or later, the day comes when I see that familiar deer-in-the-headlights look and hear the refrain: "I never expected church people to act that way!"

Make no mistake: Even as we seek to follow God's direction, we may take steps that will lead us into great hardships and difficulties. That's what happened to Paul early in his journey. Let's take a closer look as we catch up with Paul in Tarsus and the events that led up to his first missionary trip.

THE CALL

As we saw in chapter 1, Paul spent around seventeen years, mostly in Tarsus, discerning what his change in direction might mean. At the right time he would not have to go looking for opportunity; it would come looking for him in the form of an invitation from Barnabas.

Barnabas, a Jewish man from Cyprus, lived in Jerusalem. In the early days of the church he came to faith in Christ and demonstrated his commitment by selling a field and laying all the proceeds at the apostles' feet. His act inspired the disciples to begin calling him "Barnabas," which means "son of encouragement" (Acts 4:37).

Stories in Acts reveal that Barnabas shared his gift of encouragement with Paul numerous times. When the apostles refuse to meet with Paul, thinking his change in direction is a sham, Barnabas convinces them otherwise (Acts 9:27). When Jewish leaders in Jerusalem try to kill Paul for his conversion, Barnabas is among a group that puts Paul on a boat and sends him back to Tarsus (Acts 9:30). When, at the behest of the apostles, Barnabas begins serving as a leader of a thriving Christian community in Antioch of Syria, he knows who can help him. And so he extends the fateful invitation that finally launches Paul into ministry (Acts 11:22-26).

Before Barnabas enters Paul's life, do you think Paul might have felt that God had forgotten him? Seventeen years is a long time. What temptations may have crossed his mind simply to strike out on his own before he was ready—or even to abandon his path? Surely at moments he questioned his decision to return to Tarsus. He had left a successful career path only to wind up back in his parents' house! Perhaps as he learned to listen and grow in his relationship with Jesus Christ, he knew those years were not wasted.

Best-selling business author Jim Collins tells a story about his 1994 visit to the home of Peter Drucker, the world-renowned management consultant. Collins was thirty-six at the time; Drucker was eighty-five. Lingering over a bookshelf that contained Drucker's twenty-six titles, Collins was surprised to discover Drucker wrote two-thirds of the books after he turned sixty-five! Drucker would go on to add eight more books to the count before his death in 2005.[1]

How was Drucker's output increasing at a time in life when most folks are slowing down? Had Drucker put off writing in his earlier years, or was he gaining insights into what he wanted to say? Perhaps it's true that we are never simply waiting. We are laying the ground-work for what we have yet to do.

Paul's years in Tarsus were preparing him. But I also wonder if he had any hesitations. Could he have harbored any self-doubt when a call finally came? Whatever he thought or felt, he accepted this call.

Have you ever experienced a call to serve God? Perhaps you had a Barnabas who invited you to do something significant, such as teach a class, work on a mission project, or take a leadership position. Or maybe you heard about an opportunity and in that moment something inside you said, "This is it!"

I doubt most calls are so resounding that we know to follow them beyond a shadow of doubt. In fact, we may not respond to some calls for a reason; we interpret our hesitation as a sense of unpreparedness. That is why I am so grateful for my pastor's advice to me as a teenager as I struggled with whether I was truly being called to the ministry.

"As you pursue your call," he said, "the feeling will either grow stronger or weaker, and that is how you will know." I believe that advice applies to any call, not just ordained ministry. *There's more*

Perhaps with both eagerness and uncertainty, Paul says yes and departs Tarsus to accompany Barnabas to Antioch.

THE POWER OF COMMUNITY

The direction of Paul's life changes dramatically the day he arrives in Antioch, so let's take a moment and learn about the vibrant Christian church he was about to serve. In this place the term *Christian* is first used (Acts 11:26).

While Gentiles are being welcomed into the fellowship, the founding community is made up of Jews who have left Jerusalem to escape the persecution against Christ-followers—the very same persecution that Saul (Paul) had incited. Imagine the response when Barnabas introduces their newest leader! As I mentioned in the Introduction, no doubt some in the church had family members directly harmed by Paul's actions.

These folks could easily have played it safe and sent Paul on his way. Instead, the congregation chooses to embrace Paul as a church leader. They willingly believe that people can change, that God can transform hearts and redirect lives. No wonder the church is growing. Who wouldn't want to be a part of a community that not only believes God can turn people in a new direction but also welcomes them into the fold!

I once served a church that included a number of people involved in Alcoholics Anonymous (AA). One member sponsored an African American man who was still in prison but was allowed to attend worship with his sponsor. I mention his race only because our congregation was predominantly white. It had to take great courage for this man to come that first Sunday. But people welcomed him, and soon he was ushering and helping with the services.

One Sunday I invited the man to share his story during the sermon. He revealed to the congregation that he was still in prison on a violent offense. He said he came to faith while serving his sentence and through AA he was finding hope. At his conclusion, the congregation stood in applause. I felt proud of the church. Overwhelmed with emotion, the man sat down next to me. I asked if he was okay. "This is the first time," he said through tears, "that I feel forgiven."

A church that helps people feel forgiven will always be a place folks want to go. I think Antioch was just such a place.

Antioch also is the place where Paul receives another call while worshiping and fasting with the church leaders. Together they sense the Holy Spirit say, "Set apart for me Barnabas and Saul for the work to which I have called them" (Acts 13:2). They understand the Spirit to be calling the two to go out and start other churches like the one in Antioch.

Of course, God can speak to us when we are alone, but notice that the new call to Paul and Barnabas comes in the midst of community. While solitude forms an indispensable part of spiritual growth and connection to God, it doesn't replace the need for community. In community we use our gifts and discover more ways that God can use us. It's where we experience God speaking to us, challenging us, changing us. Everything Paul would go on to do results from his involvement in the Antioch church.

I imagine Paul brimming with excitement as he sets out to plant new churches like that at Antioch, anticipating the way people will welcome his efforts. Or will they?

THE REALITY OF FOLLOWING GOD'S DIRECTION

Paul and Barnabas head to Asia Minor, first sailing to Cyprus, where they meet the proconsul of Paphos and a Jewish sorcerer named Bar-Jesus. (This anecdote marks the first time Acts uses the name "Paul.") When the proconsul asks to learn more about Paul and Barnabas's faith, the sorcerer tries to discourage the conversation. Paul is "filled with the Holy Spirit" (Acts 13:0); he rebukes the sorcerer for resisting God and states that the Lord will strike him blind. When this actually comes to pass, the proconsul believes! Wouldn't you?

Let me quickly outline what happens during the rest of the first journey. From Cyprus, Paul and Barnabas go to the mainland of Asia Minor (south-central Turkey today) and come to Antioch of Pisidia, where people throng to hear them. But jealous Jewish leaders stir up opposition, and the duo find themselves expelled from the region.

Next they travel to Iconium. They receive positive response to their preaching, but again Jewish leadership creates such resistance that a plot forms to stone the two missionaries to death. Paul and Barnabas flee to Lystra, where once more they meet with a positive reception. When Paul heals a man who has never walked, the crowds declare Paul and Barnabas to be Greek gods "come down to us in human form!" (Acts 14:12). Paul corrects them, but soon, detractors from Antioch and Iconium arrive. They manage to turn the public mood, and Paul is stoned and dragged out of the city. He would have been left to die had it not been for "disciples" (Acts 14:20), probably new converts, who nurse him back to health.

Do you notice a pattern here? Opposition, expulsion, resistance, stoning. Paul and Barnabas announce the hope of new life through Jesus Christ and work to form communities where all people are welcome—and this is what they get?

This first missionary journey ends with the two missionaries retracing their path and encouraging the new believers in the towns they have previously visited. But after they sail back to Antioch of Syria, Paul and Barnabas reflect on the negative reactions when they say, "We must go through many hardships to enter the kingdom of God" (Acts 14:22, NIV). Later, in his second letter to the Corinthians, Paul recalls this period and admits, "We were under great pressure, far beyond our ability to endure, so that we despaired even of life" (1:8, NIV).

If you were Paul, would you have kept going after that first journey? Would you have even kept your faith? Wouldn't you have wondered why you experienced so much adversity if what you were doing was so right?

We all want to have the choice that Lot had when Abraham allowed him to pick between a fertile valley and a lifeless desert. Who doesn't want God to lead us where the grass is always greener? But God calls us to go where God needs us. Adversity is part of the path, not a sign we've gone the wrong way. This understanding is key to our knowledge of God's direction for our lives.

God doesn't change the world through people who play it safe. God changes the world through people willing to pick up a cross, follow a crucified Savior, and endure the trials.

THE MYTH OF EASY OBEDIENCE

As you seek to know God's direction for your life, there are a couple more points to take away from Paul's lesson.

Somewhere in modern Christianity, a strain of thought has crept in that faithfulness and comfort belong together. Maybe it's a result of the prosperity gospel that has been so popular since the 1970s. Maybe it's the need for religion to be an asylum from so much of the world's pain. But some perceive adversity as a sign that we cannot be going the way God wants. If that's the case, try telling it to Moses at the Red Sea, Elijah in the wilderness, Jesus on the cross—and, yes, to a weary Paul on the road back to Antioch.

This tension gets at the heart of our theology of pain and suffering. We may believe suffering is part of God's will and work, but allowing ourselves to embrace it is another matter.

I'm reminded of a memorable sermon that a pastor preached about Jesus' mother, Mary, in which he posed the question, "Was she the first to be asked?" The sermon pondered the possibility that the angel Gabriel may have gone to other potential candidates before Mary, but they declined once they considered the challenges and heartaches they would suffer. Mary, of course, answered unequivocally: "Let it be with me according to your word" (Luke 1:38).

Who knows what directions open up when we choose to reject the myth of easy obedience. In the words of Martin Luther King Jr., "The end of life is not to be happy. The end of life is not to achieve pleasure and avoid pain. The end of life is to do the will of God, come what may."[2]

THE BLESSING OF OPEN-ENDED PRAYERS

Frank Laubach, the Christian missionary who created a global ministry to address illiteracy, had a simple prayer he offered every morning: "God, what are you doing in the world today that I can help you with?"[3] Now that's an open-ended prayer. If you want to get serious—as Paul did—about following God's direction, look around and see where God is going. *Eccl 7:13*

Sometimes, I'll admit, I don't have a problem knowing which way God wants me to go. My problem is getting God to go in the direction I want. But as C. S. Lewis wrote in *The Great Divorce*: "There are only two kinds of people in the end: those who say to God, 'Thy will be done,' and those to whom God says, '*Thy* will be done.'"[4] *Chronicles*

We do have free will. God lets us choose the direction we want to go. But if we accept that God's way may not always be easy and if we remain open to a direction other than the one we feel inclined to take, then we have raised our spiritual antennae high.

Paul's letter to Philemon is the apostle's shortest work in the New Testament—just one chapter and fewer than five hundred words in its English translation. This letter presents Paul at his most selfless as he follows God's way. Written on behalf of a runaway slave named Onesimus, the letter is addressed to the slave's owner, Philemon, and it seeks full reconciliation between the two. Readers can deduce from the letter's pleas that Paul holds great affection for Onesimus, who has become a Christian. "So if you consider me your partner, welcome him as you would welcome me," Paul wrote. "If he has wronged you in any way, or owes you anything, charge that to my account" (Philemon 1:17-18).

Heartfelt and impassioned, the letter takes on great poignancy when we realize that Paul writes from a prison cell. He could have turned inward, settling into despondency. But even in this dire circumstance, his fate and freedom in the hands of his captors, Paul has made peace with adversity. He desires only to live an obedient life.

I recently heard about the funeral of a church member who had come to faith in middle age. This decision changed everything about his life—a fact that his wife pressed home when she asked those gathered "to say with me my husband's motto for living." The shouts rang out: "Lord, lead me where you need me!"

No doubt God longs to hear these stirring words words from us. Yet they don't necessarily make it easier for us to keep going when the going gets tough. Let us take a moment to consider what kept Paul going through adversity.

The Challenge of Reliance on God

Remembering the troubles experienced in that first missionary journey, Paul wrote, "As a result, we stopped relying on ourselves and learned to rely only on God, who raises the dead" (2 Cor. 1:9, NLT). I know this passage brings to mind unhelpful clichés such as "Just turn your problems over to God" or "Don't worry, God will make it all right" or "God never gives us more than we can handle." That last one is a real doozy. Besides having no biblical basis, it turns God into the perpetrator of our problems.

But what Paul says bears no resemblance to these sorts of clichés. He isn't being glib. He honestly answers how his faith got him through trials. Paul acknowledges that it took tough times to form his reliance on God. *Heb*

Think about all Paul brings to ministry as a well educated, credentialed man. His Roman citizenship no doubt opened a lot of doors that weren't available to average folks. But the trouble with being gifted is that we tend to rely on our gifts more than on our Giver.

Your profile and inventory includes your God-given strengths and opportunities, but these can also be sources of temptation that encourage self-reliance. Being gifted, God warns us, isn't enough. No matter how well you swim, if you're in water over your head, at some point you will need a life preserver.

Paul quickly discovered that following God's direction for his life meant taking on tough assignments that seemed well beyond the scope of his gifts. Yet, traveling with God, he told the Corinthians years later, means being willing to place ourselves in God's hands.

Paul encourages Timothy using his experience from his first missionary journey: "Now you have observed my teaching, my conduct, my aim in life, my faith, my patience, my love, my steadfastness, my persecutions and suffering the things that happened to me in Antioch, Iconium, and Lystra. What persecutions I endured! Yet the Lord rescued me from all of them" (2 Tim. 3:10-11). Then he concludes, "The Lord will rescue me from every evil attack" (4:18).

In his book *Fresh Wind, Fresh Fire*, Jim Cymbala describes his own epiphany about the meaning of putting ourselves in God's hands. He began pastoring Brooklyn Tabernacle in New York in the early 1970s, a time when the church was in desperate shape. Just days into his ministry Cymbala realized there wasn't enough money to pay the bills. He wanted to quit. In fact, that's what he did one Sunday night during a worship service. He got up to preach and found it impossible. He told the meager congregation he had no words, and he called for them to come to the altar and pray. As the people joined him in this time of utter despair, Cymbala noticed one man, an usher, begin to weep while he prayed. Cymbala went to comfort him, and suddenly the man confessed that he had been taking money out of the offering plate.

Cymbala considers that night to be the breakthrough of his ministry, which went on to attract thousands. "[God] can't resist those who humbly and honestly admit how desperately they need [God]," he writes. "Our weakness, in fact, makes room for God."[5]

THE DIFFERENCE BETWEEN ADVERSITY AND OBSTACLE

Paul's trials hardly lessen during his second missionary journey. In Philippi, he liberates a girl from slavery—a wonderful deed, unless you are her slave owners! They falsely accuse Paul and his traveling companion, Silas, of unlawfully disturbing the city. The two are subsequently flogged and thrown in prison.

Rather than curse their fate, Paul and Silas sing hymns in their cell. Then around midnight an earthquake causes all the prisoners' chains to loosen and the cell doors to open. A miracle to be sure and a chance for Paul and Silas to escape. But instead of running, Paul sees an opportunity to witness to the jailer, who is about to kill himself rather than face the punishment that he felt certain awaited him for the mass escape. Paul stops the man and offers assurances that no one is fleeing. He encourages him not to take his life but to give it to Jesus Christ. The jailer and his family end up being baptized. (Read Acts 16:16-34.)

Now think about that. Paul could have looked at his prison experience as an obstacle to following God's direction. When a miracle occurs, he could have used it as a chance to get back on track. Instead, Paul understands that this adversity never got him off track. Every experience, even a bad one, offers opportunities to keep following God's direction.

THE ABILITY OF GOD TO BRING
GOOD OUT OF BAD

Perhaps Paul's most famous line is Romans 8:28: "We know that all things work together for good for those who love God, who are called according to his purpose." He does not note this as a generalized statement regarding any bad that happens in life. He directs it at people who truly want to follow God's direction and, in the course of doing so, experience pain and challenge. Paul reassures us, saying that God works for good in all things. He knows this to be true because of his personal experience.

A jailer comes to faith because of Paul's imprisonment. A proconsul believes as a result of a sorcerer's opposition. Even Paul's own persecution of Christ-followers creates a scattering of believers who start a congregation that the transformed Paul will one day help lead! Paul believes God works for good in all things because it is proven to him, over and over again. *God the perpetrator?*

My Sunday school teacher was right. Sometimes doing good can create conflict for us. But I would add this: God can use conflict to give us new direction, and God can bring about something better than had the conflict never existed at all.

Paul wrote, "Suffering produces endurance, and endurance produces character, and character produces hope, and hope does not disappoint us" (Rom. 5:3-4).

What do you say?

SERVANT SPOTLIGHT

Patsy Wilson Tells Her Story

I believe each of us has a story to tell. Mine is a story of redemption, love, and peace.

As a young child, my sisters and I realized we were all being molested by our step-grandfather—an active pastor well known within our community. Fearfully we decided we must tell our mother. Gathered privately, we told our story and waited quietly for our mother's response. Her words sting even now for the child inside the grandmother I am now. "We will never speak of this again. We will do nothing to harm this man's reputation in the community."

We were never to know what happened among the adults after that; we do know he continued to be warmly accepted into our family gatherings and that he continued his sick actions toward us children.

My teenage and young adult years were filled with the fallout of childhood, yet throughout all of these years godly women found their way to me. They guided and hugged and listened. God was shaping me, turning the fear and betrayal into a lifelong passion for children.

It was not an easy task to work through the emotional trauma in my early life, yet God used it in a miraculous way. An organization was born out of my passion for and awareness of hurting children. Solace for the Children is dedicated to the children of war-torn countries, particularly Afghanistan. The children there find themselves ignored and hated, left uneducated and without advocates to guide them to peace and love. Serving thousands of children, Solace for the Children offers medical treatment and education. Children are brought to the United States annually to live with families who have been screened. While here they receive surgeries and treatments that are unavailable at home. Solace offers peace and love that bloom into service for others and goals for a lifetime of goodness and life.

God turned evil into good in my life. Through all of the adversity suffered by me and the children I now serve, God is present—offering health and peace and love. Trust God!

Reflection Questions

- When have you felt forgotten by God?
- How have you persevered through struggles to find and fulfill God's call on your life?
- How has the myth of easy obedience manifested in your life?
- When have you relied too much on your gifts, thereby feeding an unhealthy sense of self-reliance?
- What sustains you through times of adversity?
- When has God brought good into your life out of a bad situation? What happened?

4

DEALING WITH DETOURS

Very few persons have a chance to live their lives on the basis of their first choice. We all have to live upon the basis of our second and third choices.

— Harry Emerson Fosdick

"We know that all that happens to us is working for our good if we love God and are fitting into [God's] plans."

—Romans 8:28, *The Living Bible*

Well-known radio evangelist David Jeremiah has admitted to including a popular legend about the early days of Thomas Road Baptist Church in his sermons.[1] (Yeah, it's true. Most ministers like to recycle paper, aluminum, and sermon illustrations.)

Based in Lynchburg, Virginia, Thomas Road—now a megachurch with more than twenty thousand members—used to operate a bus ministry, picking up youth who otherwise had no way to worship and bringing them to what was then its downtown location.

As the story goes, some of the kids figured out they could come to Sunday school and then sneak out before the service to play downtown. When church deacons noticed what was happening, they stationed themselves outside to catch the wayward kids and bring them into the sanctuary. One Sunday morning, a deacon walked in with two boys in tow and plunked them down on the front row.

The sermon was especially powerful that day, and the boys listened intently. When an invitation was extended to accept Christ as Savior, both of the boys responded, and the deacons led them off after church to get baptized. As Jeremiah tells it, after the first baptism, one of the deacons said, "Son, we're going to have to get someone to take you home. I'm sure your buses have already left." The boy said, "Bus? We don't know nothing about no bus. We were walking by the church today. Some guy grabbed us and brought us into church."

Sometimes we may not get where we meant to go, but where we end up turns out better than where we were headed.

In the last chapter we examined what it means to face adversity as a result of following God's direction. In this chapter we will consider what it means to feel detoured from the direction we thought God would take us. How do we respond when we don't get to live out our purpose the way we thought we would?

Let's begin with this idea: God calls us to a purpose before God calls us to a place. I say this because I know that purpose and place can get tangled. Parents may assume their role means rearing their children in a certain home, neighborhood, and town. A teacher's sense of calling may be tied to a particular school or classroom. A job dismissal can make anyone question God's providence.

It's difficult to separate God's direction for our lives from the actual coordinates of places where we experience God using us. The greater the meaning we find in life, the more importance we attach to the place, people, and circumstances we associate with that meaning. When surroundings change, we may feel like God's purpose takes on a mechanical voice that says, "Recalculating."

Have you ever been someplace where you wonder, *How can I use my gifts here?* Have you ever found yourself in a spot that is not where you thought God would lead you? Have you ever been in a place where you simply felt lost? If so, did you realize that place has a name? It's called Troas.

An Unwanted Destination

Paul never planned to go to Troas. An Aegean coastal city located in the region of Mysia, Troas is where Paul found himself when God didn't take him where he wanted to go.

Just to recap: After his first missionary journey, Paul returned to Antioch with Barnabas and reported on their successes. If they thought, however, that their problems lay behind them, they had a reality check waiting. Previously, their problems had come from outside the church. Now, they come from the inside!

News reaches the apostles in Jerusalem that Gentiles are being brought into the church, and the apostles demand that Paul and Barnabas come to explain themselves. These original Christ-followers still identified themselves as Jewish, which meant practicing circumcision, dietary restrictions, and sabbath laws. If Christ's church was going to be open to Gentiles, then shouldn't they have to follow the same rules?

Diversity has always been a challenge in the church. Racial inclusivity has been an ongoing struggle. As Martin Luther King Jr. once observed, "Eleven o'clock on Sunday morning is one of the most segregated hours, if not the most segregated hours [sic], in Christian America."[2] Many have struggled with women's growing roles in church leadership. Now we wrestle with full inclusion for gay men, lesbians, bisexuals, and transgender people.

Perhaps this episode described in Acts can teach us a lesson.

When Paul and Barnabas are called to account in Jerusalem, they persuasively report how the Holy Spirit is given equally to Gentiles and Jews in the congregations they start. In the end, the council, believing God wants everyone to be a part of the church, amends requirements once held sacred. Certain Jewish laws no longer had to be strictly observed to follow Christ.

Having won that battle, Paul and Barnabas return to Antioch, where they intend to launch a second trip, retracing their previous steps to share the news from Jerusalem. That is the plan until their dispute over Mark, Barnabas's cousin, arises. Mark actually traveled with Paul and Barnabas for a time on the first journey, but he returned home early from that trip. Paul perceived him as undependable and refuses to take him on this second journey. Paul and Barnabas get into such a heated argument that they go their separate ways. Barnabas and Mark sail to Cyprus. Paul leaves with Silas to visit the churches started on the first journey.

From there, Paul wants to go north to the region of Bithynia, a densely populated province of the Roman Empire. Why Bithynia? Paul probably believes its residents will be receptive to the Christian message. In fact, a letter written sixty years after Paul's time by a Bithynian official to the Roman emperor states that Christianity was thriving in the cities and outlying areas.

No wonder Paul wants to go there. Clearly success awaits him. Most of us want to go in the direction of success. After all, if we want to make a positive impact for God, we can safely assume that God will take us where it looks like that will happen. We don't expect God to send us where the chance of success seems limited.

Paul sets his sights on a place where he can make the greatest impact for the gospel. He encounters only one problem: God has other ideas! "When they had come opposite Mysia," the book of Acts reports, "they attempted to go into Bithynia, but the Spirit of Jesus did not allow them; so, passing by Mysia, they went down to Troas" (16:7-8).

At this point, I think Paul's years of preparation in Arabia and Tarsus pay off. The time he has spent learning to listen to Christ means he can determine that God is putting up a roadblock. Has that ever happened to you? Have you ever strongly desired something, but after many obstacles you began to wonder if God was saying, "I don't want you to go that way"? How do you determine that God is telling you to hold up?

No one can answer that for you. You have to do your own listening, discerning, and interpreting. But I do know this: If we wait until we come to the fork in the road to listen to God, we may feel like we're having a conversation with a bad cell phone connection. The call keeps getting dropped.

In my own life I tend to be more open to receiving God's directions when I'm not peppering God with questions, desperate for answers. Whatever message Paul receives, he is certain of one fact: Bithynia is not in the plans. Thus he ends up in a place he never intended to be, Troas, wondering what will come next.

Let's consider what detours can teach us about finding God's direction for our lives.

OPPORTUNITIES IN NEW PLACES

Any disappointment Paul may have felt in skipping Bithynia passes quickly. Notice what happens once Paul lands in Troas:

> During the night Paul had a vision: there stood a man of Macedonia pleading with him and saying, "Come over to Macedonia and help us." When he had seen the vision, we immediately tried to

cross over to Macedonia, being convinced that God had called us
to proclaim the good news to them. (Acts 16:9-10)

As a side note, this is the first time the book of Acts uses the first-
person plural, we, which indicates that Luke, the author, is a traveling
companion with Paul. And don't miss the significance of the vision.
By pursuing it, Paul and his companions introduce the gospel to the
European continent. Jesus' instruction to the disciples to be his "wit-
nesses . . . to the ends of the earth" (Acts 1:8) is about to take a big
step in the right direction.

When have you felt challenged to dream anew? Actually, new
dreams often aren't the biggest challenge. Letting go of old ones is.
In his Gospel, Luke records Jesus saying, "No one who puts a hand
to the plow and looks back is fit for the kingdom of God" (9:62).
I don't believe that means Jesus rejects people who hesitate or have
second thoughts. Rather, I believe Jesus simply states that it's hard to
embrace new opportunities when we can't let go of past dreams.

Paul has an uncanny ability not to dwell on the past or what
might have been. In a new place, perhaps even an unwanted place, he
quickly turns the page and prays, "Lord, how can you use me here?"
We see this spirit in his letter to the Philippians, "This one thing I do:
forgetting what lies behind and straining forward to what lies ahead,
I press on toward the goal for the prize of the heavenly call of God in
Christ Jesus" (3:13-14).

After Martin Luther King Jr. completed his doctoral class work at
Boston University in 1954, he set out to secure a pulpit and received
invitations to preach trial sermons at two churches. One was in Chattanooga, Tennessee, the other in Montgomery, Alabama. King really
wanted to go to the Chattanooga church, which was considered a little
more prestigious, but he was passed over. The Montgomery church,
Dexter Avenue Baptist, offered an invitation and he accepted.[3]

King could have gone there thinking, *If only.* . . . He could have gone looking for the first opportunity to move on to a better place, but he made himself fully available in his Troas and let God use him in any capacity.

In December 1955, eighteen months after King had arrived, Rosa Parks defied segregation laws and refused to sit in the back of a city bus. After her arrest and jailing, local African American leaders organized and launched a bus boycott. King was chosen as the group's president. The successful boycott and King's role in it is considered to be the catalyst for the modern Civil Rights Movement.

We are most open to receiving God's direction when we pray, "Lord, how can you use me here?"

DOORS IN DETOURS

Failing to let go of a dream can keep us from embracing new opportunities, but failing to let go of our own best-laid plans can do the same. Failing to plan is planning to fail, but a rigid determination to stick to a plan can crowd out opportunities for God to use us.

Writing to the Corinthians, Paul talked about a time in his third missionary journey: "I do not want to see you now just in passing, for I hope to spend some time with you, if the Lord permits. But I will stay in Ephesus until Pentecost, for a wide door for effective work has opened to me, and there are many adversaries" (1 Cor. 16:7-9).

Clearly Paul has planned to visit Corinth, but he realizes God is presenting him with opportunities in Ephesus. So he adjusts his plans. Once more we see the benefit of Paul's time spent listening to God in preparation for his life as a missionary. He remains open to God's saying, "Not so fast! Adjust your plan. I can do more with you here than where you want to go next."

Driving down an interstate highway one day I saw an electronic road sign that read PLAN FOR DELAYS. Of course, my stomach sank. I didn't have time for delays. I thought, *I could have planned for a delay—if I'd known earlier!* Then I pondered how often God sends me the same message. Do I build into my life the freedom for God to say, "Before you hurry off to the next item on your agenda, I want to use you in this moment. Can you build allowance into your schedule for me to use you now?" Sometimes what we experience as delays are really God's way of opening a new door to us.

A few years ago, I was serving a church in suburban Charlotte, North Carolina, when Compassion International, a nonprofit organization that serves children in poverty contacted my associate pastor, Andrea Smith. The organization asked Andrea if our church would participate in a pilot project connecting American congregations with places of great need in the world. She had several places to consider, so she and the chair of the missions committee prayed about it and felt God leading them to choose India.

The two made a scouting trip to an Indian village and returned with excitement about what our church could do. A group of church members was recruited for a mission trip. Then, only weeks before departure, Compassion International called with disappointing news: Because of unexpected stumbling blocks, it was unable to continue its link to India.

The mission group members felt devastated. What would they do now? In their distress, Andrea and the committee chair went to prayer. If God was leading them, then surely God had another idea.

As the group prayed in the church office, Andrea's cell phone rang. The caller was from Samaritan's Feet, a ministry based in Charlotte that works to provide shoes to the needy around the world. Our church had conducted a recent shoe-packing event for the group, and now it needed a team to go to Uganda.

"Would you be willing?" the caller asked.

Two weeks later, the mission team was on the ground in the jungles of Uganda. There they met two young men, pastors who were doing all they could to raise children orphaned by the AIDS crisis. The two pastors showed the group around the village and then took them to an open field.

"This is it," one said.

"This is what?" Andrea asked.

"The place you will build the huts."

"What huts?"

"The new huts to provide housing for the children."

Then the pastors displayed the plans they had for the buildings. The cost would be $10,000 per hut.

"Wait a minute," Andrea said. "We just came to deliver shoes. We didn't commit to building huts!"

"Sure you will," said the pastors. "We've prayed about this. We asked God to send us someone to help us build the huts, and you arrived."

"I'm sure you did," Andrea said, "but. . . ."

The chair of the missions committee interrupted her. "When did you pray?" she asked the two pastors.

They recalled the exact day and time.

Andrea pulled out her cell phone. The call she received from Samaritan's Feet came at the same time on the same day—even accounting for the time zone difference!

The Sunday after they returned from Uganda, I shared their story with the congregation. Six months later, another mission team returned to construct two huts and start two more.

Some detours are really doors of opportunity.

FEAR OF TAKING WRONG PATHS

When you study Paul's life you don't get the sense he did much hand-wringing or asking people, "What do you think?" He was not impetuous or indifferent. He just lived with a freedom from compulsive worry over whether he had made the right decision.

One of the great reflections on decision making is Robert Frost's poem "The Road Not Taken," even though its meaning is still being debated a century after it was written, particularly its last line: "I took the one less traveled by, And that has made all the difference."[4]

Some say the poem is an appeal to live free of other people's expectations and demands, as if the choice lies between a popular path and a true path. Some dispute that interpretation, pointing out Frost says the users of both paths "had worn them really about the same." Still others say the poem encourages people not to follow only the enticing paths. But that interpretation is questioned because Frost says both were "just as fair."

So what's the point?

Perhaps Frost was simply acknowledging the reality that we all struggle with the temptation to relive key choices in life and wonder if we made the right decisions.

Paul seems to have lived free of second-guessing. He knew that no path removes us from God's direction. When we understand that God can guide us on whichever path we choose at a fork, then we are freer to make informed decisions. Paul felt less concern about making strategic choices than living in the truth of who God called him to be. His purpose, if you will, was to be his true self, to live out his identity in Christ whatever path he was on.

DETOURS' HIDDEN POTENTIAL

We can find it daunting when we find ourselves headed in a new, unexpected direction. How can we possibly embrace a detour? By believing that God will do something better with us.

The modern city of Kavala, Greece, is located along the far northern edge of the Aegean Sea near the borders of Bulgaria and Turkey. In Paul's day, it fell within the state of Macedonia and was called Neapolis. Paul arrives in this city following his vision in Troas.

Today a beautiful mosaic in the town depicts this story. No other memorials like this exist in the places Paul visited on his first missionary journey. Neapolis is where Paul becomes a truly historic figure. In Neapolis—a place he never intended to go—a detour turned out for the best.

As you seek to follow God's direction for your life, trust that you are never beyond God's ability to guide. In fact, to God, there's no such thing as a detour. Think about it: A detour simply means we aren't pursuing the route we originally had in mind. Believing a detour offers a new opportunity from God can encourage us to welcome these possibilities.

Recall missionary Frank Laubach's daily prayer, "God, what are you doing in the world today that I can help with?"[5] this prayer came as a result of a detour. In 1915, a Christian missionary organization sent Laubach to the Philippines, where he taught at Union Theological Seminary in Manila. He was almost elected president of the seminary, missing it by one vote—the vote he cast for the other candidate!

Not long afterward, he had the opportunity to work with the Maranao tribe in the southern Philippines. Realizing that these Muslim people could not read or write, he discovered a passion that would become his all-consuming mission: literacy. The people didn't receive Laubach at first, but because of his willingness to live among them, learn their language, and listen to them, they finally received his teaching.

Church donations to mission work dried up during the Great Depression, and Laubach had no resources to keep teaching the tribe. The chieftain who learned to read and write under Laubach said, "If I can learn, anyone can learn. Let each one who learned to read teach someone else." This led to the "each one, teach one" literacy method that was eventually adopted in over a hundred countries.[6]

Laubach's work has been lauded around the world. He became known as the "Apostle to the Illiterates." Like Paul, this apostle's great work may have never been realized had it not been for a rerouting.

Sometimes we may not get where we meant to go, but where we end up turns out better than where we were headed.

Oh, and by the way, remember that argument Paul and Barnabas had over Mark? As far as we know Paul and Barnabas were never together again. But Paul did write to Timothy later in his life and say, "Bring Mark, for he is useful to me in my ministry," suggesting that Paul would reconnect with Mark. And do you recognize the name Mark? He is credited with writing one of the four Gospels. Can you say, "Thank you, God, for detours"?

SERVANT SPOTLIGHT

Francis Wyatt Tells His Story

Trust in the LORD with all your heart, and do not rely on your own insight. In all your ways acknowledge him and he will make straight your paths.

—Proverbs 3:5-6

I felt like I've heard that quote from my mother every week of my life. Growing up as an African American male in the Cochran projects of St. Louis, I found it hard to believe the possibility of her words. But I trusted and embarked on what I now acknowledge to be a very interesting journey.

When I was still a child, my mother noticed my gift for music—percussion, to be exact. I guess it began with my dragging out the pots and pans and banging on them with wooden soup spoons or creating a drum set from empty boxes in front of the complex.

Being a single parent, Mom would always seek ways for me to connect and be mentored by strong male figures. This led to my years of marching in various DCI (Drum Corp International) events over a ten-year period. Through this experience I glimpsed how much more was available to me than what the projects offered. I traveled the country, and my love for music grew. Being a racial minority in most situations, my understanding of cultural uniqueness grew . . . and I found myself appreciating and craving those opportunities to expand my understanding. That's where I learned about Rush and Def Leppard after growing up on Gap Band and Cameo!

I knew music was my vehicle to a better life. It led me into the Air Force. I served with the Band of Flight in Ohio for ten years as a percussionist. There I met my wife, Cheryl, and we adopted our two wonderful kids. I had the opportunity to play and travel with world-renowned artists, including the Joe Henderson sextet. I truly thought that was going to be my life's direction. Then God introduced a detour that rerouted me. Cheryl and I felt the call to serve the local church.

Through several Spirit-led encounters, I started out as a part-time music director at Ginghamsburg United Methodist Church in Tipp City, Ohio, and eventually became part of the full-time staff. The seven years I served there proved to be an incredibly formative experience not only as a worship leader but also as a disciple of Christ. Feeling it was time to move on, I served for a year in a predominantly black church in downtown Dayton, Ohio, a move that I now see God used to prepare us for the next seven years.

A large Chicago suburb church asked me to help start a new venue in the loop. I've always thought I had a bead on what diversity was about, but I quickly came to understand that I had much more to learn. As I grew as an individual, so did the church. I honestly thought this was the place where God was going to use me for the remainder of my journey, the place where I could bring all I am to all I know God to be. But then came another shift in direction. Changes in leadership and direction in the church led me to see this was not the place for my ongoing ministry.

A few months later I learned that a church in Indianapolis, Indiana, was starting a contemporary service and looking for a worship leader. My wife and I felt a clear call to start a contemporary service. St. Luke's United Methodist Church was known throughout the city for the quality of their traditional worship. Several phones calls, visits, and interviews later we moved to Indianapolis. These days I am constantly being made aware of how we as a people create so many subcultures. Discerning how to "reconnect" them is an incredible task, but that is the call for the unification of the body. So my wife and I rerouted our path and started the new journey.

I would love to say that I felt ready for this detour, but honestly I was not. The challenges we faced went far beyond cultural differences. There was pain, mistrust, and fear of the unknown for my family and for the church. Many times during the first two years I found myself questioning whether this was a detour or a dead end.

But time proved otherwise. This past year I've come to embrace who God is asking me to be for the sake of what God is doing at this church. I've learned not to make my ministry about me and to stay focused on what Christ wants to do through me. It reminds me of Paul's words, "To the Jews, I became as a Jew" (1 Cor. 9:20). I have realized that the church's acceptance of the contemporary service has mirrored my acceptance of the church.

In my journey with God I have often wondered, *Lord, why did you lead me here?* only to discover in hindsight that God is working not only for the good of others but for my good as well. So, have I landed? Have I taken my final journey? Or does another rerouting lie ahead? Honestly, I'm good with either call. These days I'm loving who I am . . . and where I am!

REFLECTION QUESTIONS

- When have you found yourself in a spot that is not where you thought God would lead you?
- When have you felt challenged to dream anew?
- How have you used a detour as a door of opportunity?
- How do you find freedom to live into your fullest potential?
- What is God doing in the world today that you can help with?

5

RELYING ON GOD

The psychic task which a person can and must set for himself, is not to feel secure, but to be able to tolerate insecurity.

—Erich Fromm

The Spirit God gave us does not make us timid, but gives us power, love and self-discipline.

—2 Timothy 1:7, NIV

I'm a climber. I don't know why God wired me that way, but I instinctually want to go higher. Sometimes that's gotten me into trouble. As a kid, I got my leg so wedged between two tree branches that my grandmother had to find a nearby construction worker to climb up and pry me loose.

Perhaps my most memorable misadventure occurred when my wife, Susan, and I were vacationing in Colorado with our two oldest daughters, Julie and Sarah, who were three and one at the time. One morning we decided to hike into a remote canyon that promised beautiful views. I carried Sarah on my back and when Julie got tired, I lugged her in front of me. I looked like a human pack mule, and let's leave it at that.

After several miles, we stopped for a lunch break in a quiet meadow, but as I tried to enjoy the scenery, I couldn't help feeling restless. It was as if voices, like the sirens in *The Odyssey*, were beckoning me from the cliff tops.

I told Susan I wanted to explore "for a few minutes." She said she was happy to rest and watch the girls play by the stream. Off I headed to see how high I could climb.

Somewhere in my aggressive ascent—far out of earshot—I got stuck. The only way to get past the rock above me was to hang suspended and pull myself up over it. Rock climbers call this a "dead pull." (Note to all weekend warriors: Anything preceded by the word *dead* is probably not going to lead to a stress-free experience!)

Not feeling confident enough to try that move, I looked below to see a steep slope covered by a large swath of snow, the last vestiges of winter. I knew from experience the slickness of melting snow. I had managed going up, but one little slip going down could be deadly.

For the first time in climbing, I had an unfamiliar feeling: I didn't trust myself. I didn't think I had the strength to go up or the reliable footing to go down. Staying put was not an option, even if I had any thought of somehow being rescued. I was using up my strength just to hold my position.

I stood there for what felt like a good half hour. I knew Susan was probably wondering where I was and growing impatient, perhaps even worried. Finally, I made my move, gradually inching myself sideways, clinging to every millimeter of rock. Eventually I got to a spot where I could get a foothold that allowed me to step up to a wider ledge. Soon I was able to scamper to the top of the cliff and walk down from a much safer route, though it was a longer descent.

When I reached Susan. . . . Well, let's just say it was a very quiet walk back to the car.

Have you ever stood on that mountain? The mountain of insecurity, fear, and self-doubt? Ever been in the middle of following what you believed to be God's direction for your life only to get stuck?

It's an awful place, isn't it? For one thing you risk becoming immobilized. When you lose your confidence, you become afraid to take any step. Also, getting out of an uncomfortable spot like that can create a fear of ever putting yourself in a similar situation again.

Dealing with the possibility of getting stuck recognizes an important tension in living with purpose. On one hand, we trust that God is leading us to a purpose that focuses on our gifts, abilities, and interests. Living with purpose is very much about doing the things we're good at.

On the other hand, we allow God to lead us to places where we have to utterly depend on God. Following God's direction means attempting challenges that can succeed only with God's help.

Hence the tension: Living with purpose means we may find ourselves in places where we're in over our heads. Those experiences invite one of two responses from us. We either will retreat from them, vowing never to allow ourselves to get in such a position again, or we will learn and grow from them, refusing to let insecurity control us.

Staying stuck is not an option, but what determines which way we will go when we do start to move?

EXPERIENCE A MOMENT OF CRISIS

Paul came to Athens on his second missionary journey. This had to be a bucket-list visit for someone who grew up in Tarsus, a leading university city of its day. Athens was home to the intellectual elite. If academic prowess was among your gifts, then a visit to Athens was a chance to find out just how gifted you were.

Paul enters the city on a wave of success. Granted, he's had setbacks, but those really confirmed he was going in the right direction. People stirred up opposition to Paul because of the crowds who flocked to hear him. Athens, however, will offer Paul a new experience.

Acts 17:16-34 tells the story. The number of idols placed throughout the city disturbs Paul. In fact, because of the many idols, a city ordinance made it illegal to promote a new religion without the approval of the council of philosophers. This is what got Paul into trouble.

As was his custom, Paul goes to the synagogues, where he argues and reasons his faith in Christ with both Jews and the "God-fearing" Gentiles who embrace Jewish beliefs. Paul also takes his message to the streets, preaching in the famous Agora, or marketplace.

To the philosophers, Paul's message about the resurrection of Jesus Christ advocates a new religion, which is like fishing without a license. Soon the council of philosophers summons Paul to the top of the Areopagus, or Mars Hill, a large outcropping high above the Agora and not far from the Parthenon. Now Paul has to make his case before this body, which resembles the academic supreme court.

Paul chooses a different approach in this arena. He begins by employing a popular technique in Greek rhetoric: flattering his audience. "Athenians," he said, "I see how extremely religious you are in every way" (Acts 17:22). Rather than quote scripture, he quotes Greek philosophers. He also tries to impress them with the logic of his argument, noting that one of the city's idols represents an unknown god. "What therefore you worship as unknown," he said, "this I proclaim to you" (17:23). Surely Paul must think the philosophers will find this a clever defense against the charge of advocating a new religion.

Though Paul persuades some of his listeners to become believers, many scoff at his mention of resurrection. By the end of the day, Paul has worked hard to make an intellectual appeal but finds himself laughed at for his silly ideas.

MAKE A SIGNIFICANT SHIFT

Acts 18 begins with Paul's abrupt departure from Athens for Corinth. The distance between the two is not far—about sixty miles—but it is probably one of the longest trips Paul makes in his ministry. In those miles, he has to confront the notion that he'd used all of his gifts and abilities and come away with disappointing results. *what about the "don't second guess himself"*

Imagine using all of your God-given talent to live out your purpose, but you can't see that you are making any difference. You pour all your energy and effort into teaching, but the students don't seem to care. You labor with all your might in your business, but you can't turn a profit. You give your best as a parent so your children will treat one another lovingly, but you feel you are losing the battle. You do your best to lead your church but it still doesn't grow. As the Proverb says, "Hope deferred makes the heart sick" (13:12).

How do we know Paul was probably struggling with a major bout of insecurity? Scripture does not mention that he went to counseling, attended a Tony Robbins seminar, or watched reruns of *Braveheart*. But many years after leaving Corinth, he does tell us enough to conclude that something significant is going on inside of him. In a letter to the Corinthians, he recalls his state of mind after his arrival from Athens:

> When I came to you, brothers and sisters, I did not come proclaiming the mystery of God to you in lofty words or wisdom. For I decided to know nothing among you except Jesus Christ, and him crucified. And I came to you in weakness and in fear and in much trembling. My speech and my proclamation were not with plausible words of wisdom, but with a demonstration of the Spirit

and of power, so that your faith might rest not on human wisdom but on the power of God. (1 Cor. 2:1-5)

Does that sound like a shift to you? Does that sound like someone who relied on his ability, came up short, and then found himself momentarily stuck?

Let's be clear: If this can happen to Paul, it can happen to any of us. And let me be even clearer: This experience is part of the journey of following God's direction for our lives.

God has a way of leading us to places where our abilities will fall short. That's not to say our gifts are insignificant. They play a crucial role; but no matter how gifted we are, we will have times when we grow insecure about our ability to conquer a challenge. Willingness to abandon what makes us feel secure can signal trust and faith, just as it did for Peter when Jesus beckoned him to get out of the boat and walk on water. But these moments can also lead us to second-guessing, just as it did for Peter when he doubted the miracle and began to sink. (Read Matthew 14:27-31.)

We often receive opportunities to grow—but how can we grow through a bout of insecurity? I want to offer some guidance with the help of Paul's example.

BE A FACE PERSON

Jesse Owens, son of an Alabama sharecropper, discovered he had the gift of being able to run fast. While still in high school, he set a world record in the hundred-meter dash. But he would learn that his gift had a greater purpose than just winning races. As an African American, he discovered his fame gave him the opportunity to help break down barriers of racism, and he single-handedly shattered Hitler's claim of Aryan superiority when he took home four gold medals at the 1936 Olympics in Nazi Germany.

In describing her son's ability to overcome the obstacles of his life, Mary Emma Owens said, "Jesse was always a face boy. . . . When a problem came up, he always faced it."[1]

You could say Paul was a "face boy" too. Whenever a challenge came along, he faced it. Still, I imagine it was much easier to face external challenges, such as repressive authorities and angry mobs, than the internal opponent of self-doubt. The challenger inside of us usually is the one that has the best chance of getting us to back down. Yet the response needs to be the same: Just face it!

For Paul, facing it meant returning to basics. As he said in First Corinthians, that meant relying on the power of the Holy Spirit rather than clever and persuasive speeches; it meant trusting in God's power rather than human wisdom.

No matter what our abilities, our greatest asset is our willingness to rely on God. Spiritual dependence always trumps self-reliance—a truth that runs contrary to the ways of the world. Ambition, talent, leadership, independence: Society tends to value these traits. But the measurement of our greatest success will be our willingness to depend on God. This principle applies to all who seek to follow God's direction for their lives. God will routinely put us in a place where we must ask ourselves, "What am I relying on most right now, my ability or God's?"

Abraham knew that place well. He displayed his willingness to depend on God when he followed God's direction to leave his homeland. But that first difficult step of faith didn't guarantee that the next steps would come any easier. Time and again, Abraham struggled with insecurity. When he and his wife, Sarah, fled a famine and traveled to Egypt, he persuaded Sarah to pass herself off as his sister. The lie, he believed, would keep the Egyptians from killing him and stealing her for her beauty. It did little good. Pharaoh still took Sarah into his palace, causing God to step in and send plagues to his household. That got Pharaoh's attention! Once he learned the truth about Sarah, he returned her to Abraham. (Read Genesis 12:10-20.) What was the point? We never stop needing God to step in!

When Abraham and Sarah at last had a promised son, Isaac, God called Abraham to take the boy to Mount Moriah and sacrifice him. This story remains one of the most challenging stories in scripture to understand. It is full of troubling ideas, not the least of which is the use of child sacrifice as a test of faith. But for God and Abraham, there was a need to know. Would Abraham rely on his gift more than on God?

When we aren't willing to depend on God, we make whatever we do for God about us—about our own need to succeed or to gain others' approval or to chase away our own insecurities. Truthfully, God is always more concerned with our character than our accomplishments.

A good faith question to ask from time to time is this: What am I doing that requires God to step in?

KNOW YOURSELF

Where are you most likely to get stuck? Understanding what drives you gives you insight into knowing the answer to that question.

We often talk about Type A and Type B personalities, but a prevailing school of thought in popular psychology agrees that four major types exist: A, B, C, and D.[2]

Type As like to be in charge and in control of their environment. They tend to be driven and goal-oriented. Type As experience frustration when they have no clear goal and when time is wasted.

Type Bs differ from As in that they are not easily stressed and not motivated by deadlines. Connecting with people is a driving need.

Type Cs tend to be introverts who like details and control. They are drawn to figuring things out logically. They like working with facts and figures more than people.

Last, the Type D personality type prefers sticking to the known and proven. Instability and change are huge stressors for this type.

While no one is solely one type, we all tend toward one.

Knowing your personality type will help you understand where you're most likely to get stuck in a place of insecurity. For instance, because Type As are driven by the need to get things done, they are more likely to bail on a mission when they can't produce the desired results. Rather than taking time to pray and lean on God for understanding, they will face the temptation to jump to another assignment that offers the lure of quick gain.

Type Bs can get stuck most easily in isolation. Think of Elijah so quickly feeling insecure, tired, and alone in the wilderness even after he had single-handedly stood down the four hundred and fifty prophets of Baal. (See 1 Kings 18–19.)

Type C personalities may get stuck when solutions aren't forthcoming. Being gifted at problem solving, they may overcompensate in the face of uncertainty by trying to exert control and stability.

Finally, Type Ds may get stuck simply trying to get started. Playing it safe is their default setting so the mere presence of risk can paralyze them. Consider the other disciples in the boat and how they probably felt when Peter got out.

In knowing yourself, what tends to make you insecure? Think about the last time you felt that way. In that experience, how could you have practiced reliance on the Holy Spirit?

In Corinth, Paul recalibrates his focus on the Holy Spirit, returning to the practices he had developed during his seventeen years post-conversion. He abandons being clever and persuasive for the plain, unimpressive willingness to preach reliance on the crucified Christ.

Make no mistake: The posture of total surrender doesn't look heroic; but to God, this is when we are at our best. I know how good it feels when people tell me I've preached well. I'm sure God smiles too, but God's pleasure also encompasses the days leading up to those

Sundays when I feel utterly helpless and pray in desperation for God to give me words to say. I have noticed that the sermons that get the most positive responses are the ones I've prayed the hardest over.

Could it be that the places God wants to lead us are the places that will make us most dependent?

AVOID COMPARISONS

This may sound odd but I'm more drawn to confident losers than confident winners. Sure, it's appealing to hear a quarterback after a game-winning touchdown say, "I knew I was going to make that pass." Yeah, I figure he probably did. That's what makes him a winner.

But then I listen to the losing quarterback who says, "I gave it my best. We came up short, but I look forward to another chance against that team!" For some reason I am more drawn to that person—not because I am more familiar with coming up short but because I know my tendency to make excuses. We've all heard those post-game interviews: "That bad call really hurt us" . . . "My knee injury slowed me down" . . . "The other team just got some lucky breaks." I am drawn to the person who accepts defeat without excuse and uses it as a chance to improve.

Those traits are rare in a culture where winning, losing, and succeeding are based on how we compare to others. Often, when we want to feel better about ourselves, we feel tempted to make ourselves appear better than those around us. Pioneering psychotherapist Alfred Adler describes this as "striving for superiority," the need to make others feel inferior in order to feel secure about ourselves.[3]

Insecurity can drive behaviors as much as our personality types do. People insecure in social settings may talk too much. People insecure about their own standing may come off as braggarts. People insecure about their appearance may obsess over what they wear.

What situations tend to make you most insecure? In what ways do you overcompensate?

Paul has probably seen a fair amount of this behavior in his time. In Second Corinthians, he writes, "When they measure themselves by one another, and compare themselves with one another, they do not show good sense" (10:12). Often our insecurity is not about our failure or fear of failure but our fear that we won't do as well as someone else. We begin to measure our success against what others have done. Falling short in such comparisons can bring feelings of inadequacy.

When those feelings arise, we need to recognize our own uniqueness. Comparing ourselves to others is really comparing how we would do in their place. Instead, God is calling you to your place. As Paul wrote, "All must test their own work; then that work, rather than their neighbor's work, will become a cause for pride" (Gal. 6:4). God asks us to start with the belief that no matter our circumstances, God will use us where we are.

The next step comes in allowing failure to be part of the process of our discovering what God wants to do. If you are like me, a Type A/Type C personality, that's a hard thing to allow. Failing never feels okay, but getting better does. I have to remind myself that failure makes me a better person. I learn more from my failures than my successes. I grow more when I acknowledge that I need to improve my game. The key is not worrying about what others will think of my failure or how it will appear.

Finally, making a point to celebrate others' successes helps slay the giant of comparison. When colleagues' accomplishments make you envious, write them a note of congratulation, even if you don't know them well. Tell them of your admiration for their work and offer your thanks for their example. When you talk with others, be intentional about getting to know them. Draw attention to the celebrations in their lives. These are little ways to break free of the inner demon of measuring ourselves against others.

Once more Paul advises, "That means we will not compare ourselves with each other as if one of us were better and another worse. We have far more interesting things to do with our lives. Each of us is an original" (Gal. 5:25-26, THE MESSAGE).

PUT OBEDIENCE FIRST

Last of all, remember that God calls us to be obedient, not successful. The measure of success comes in our *seeking* God rather than in our *serving* God.

On the day of Pentecost, a small group of people were doing what Jesus told them—staying in the city until they received power from God. They prayed and waited. Obedience preceded power. And then the Holy Spirit arrived, and three thousand came to faith.

Three thousand! That's an impressive number, isn't it?

But imagine, if you will, that God had gathered another group simultaneously in, say, Jericho, and four thousand people came to faith. Yes, we'd celebrate the grand total of seven thousand, but we'd probably also start to measure the significance based on the results. Wouldn't you perhaps wonder what happened in Jericho that maybe didn't happen in Jerusalem?

Today we know so much about the measurement of God's work at churches in specific places—Chicago, Dallas, Seattle—that we spend more time studying them than we do focusing on Jerusalem. I have the frequent flyer miles to prove it!

When I turn to Jerusalem, I feel called to pay attention most to the disciples' obedience.

I'm not recommending that we discard benchmarking. I am a great proponent of learning from others, especially those who are experiencing positive outcomes. But when I visit churches doing ministry well, what I invariably learn is that they look like the group in Jerusalem. Most of them teach the same lesson: Practice obedience! We can learn from anyone, but no example and no lesson will take the place of our turning to God for help, instruction, and empowerment.

Paul arrived in Athens and perhaps made his mission about himself. Once in Corinth, he decided to make his mission about Christ.

Paul's ministry did not focus on his success or ability to convert people. Only God can do that. Paul's job? Be obedient and preach the truth of the crucified savior. God used him in ways that he could never have imagined.

What does God imagine for you?

Servant Spotlight

Bethany Garrity Tells Her Story

For years, I came to church week after week, year after year, to listen to the sermon, pick up the kids from Sunday school, and go home. It was comfortable. As a wife and mother of two young boys, a director for a national fitness company, as well as a student working on my master's in business administration, I didn't have time for more. But along the way I felt God tugging at me to look outside of what I needed church to do for me. I conveniently pushed aside the nudges I felt in worship by the time I got to the car, consumed with what awaited me at home or work. Most weeks, I congratulated myself that I attended church.

August of 2014, however, was a game changer. I don't recall any specific requests from the pulpit. I just remember being overwhelmed with an impulse to step into something unknown, something that would allow me to spread God's love to others. I sent an e-mail to the pastors of my church saying, "Enough already! I'm through pretending church is for me exclusively. Use me."

Eventually I met with our missions pastor. She listed a few things she had in mind for outreach, and when she described a program called Getting Ahead, I felt sure that was where I needed to be spending my volunteer time. Getting Ahead helps individuals living in poverty climb out of their circumstances as volunteers *walk with* people rather than *do for* them. Volunteers provide support, resources, and connection for those who choose to work and improve their situations.

I translated this volunteer work into orchestrating what needed to be done in the background to make a difference in Getting Ahead. Because that's where I'm comfortable . . . in the background. Being in relationship with people in poverty was far from my comfort zone. Talk about feeling insecure! I didn't know anything about poverty. *How could I help people?* I knew I would be better suited to supporting others on the front line. I soon found out that when God calls us to follow, we don't always determine the direction!

REFLECTION QUESTIONS

- When have you followed what you believed to be God's direction for your life only to get stuck?

- What situations tend to make you feel most insecure? In what ways do you overcompensate?

- How have you grown through a bout of insecurity?

- When have you had to choose between relying on God's ability or on your own? Reflect on that situation.

- What are you doing that requires God to step in?

- What is God imagining for you?

6

DEVELOPING TENACITY

Fall seven times, stand up eight.

—Japanese proverb

[God] will also strengthen you to the end.

—1 Corinthians 1:8, NLT

When the time came in 1964 for Nelson Mandela to defend himself against charges of trying to overthrow the South African government, the forty-five-year-old activist chose to make a statement against apartheid rather than present evidence to clear his name. For three hours in a Pretoria court, Mandela masterfully articulated his reasons for acting against the state-sponsored system of segregation, oppression, and discrimination. He concluded with these words:

During my lifetime I have dedicated myself to this struggle of the African people. I have fought against white domination, and I have fought against black domination. I have cherished the ideal of a democratic and free society in which all persons live together in harmony and with equal opportunities. It is an ideal which I hope to live for and to achieve. But if need be, it is an ideal for which I am prepared to die.[1]

The address became known as Mandela's "I am prepared to die" speech. He had already served two years in prison, and now he would serve another twenty-six. Four years after his release in 1990, he was elected president of South Africa.

Mandela clearly had a sense of purpose and destiny. He expressed a commitment to the cause of freedom for all people, a cause for which he was prepared to die. In determining what was worth dying for, he found what he was meant to live for.

Mandela, the son of a tribal chieftain, expected to assume his father's position. He was destined for leadership. Yet, he chose to forgo that role to take up the cause of liberation for black South Africans. He was also a Christian who was baptized as a Methodist. He attended a Methodist school as a child and though largely quiet about his faith once he became president, it still played a critical role in his life. One of his most famous quotes reflects a fundamental Christian ethic, "Until I changed myself, I could not change others."[2]

Consider the significance of this conviction when Mandela, as president, dealt with countless black South Africans desiring revenge against the whites who had caused so much pain and abuse.

I have wondered what kept Mandela going in his years of suffering. Could he possibly have imagined a day when he would head a government that once deemed him an enemy of the state? What kept him from giving up during those long, difficult years in prison? What kept him from abandoning his ideals as he endured his jailers' daily abuse? What would have been different had Mandela not persevered?

Sometimes following God's direction in our lives comes down to tenacity, a willingness not to give up and to believe that a persevering spirit will prevail. As Alexander Graham Bell, the inventor of the telephone, once said of his own perseverance, "What this power is I cannot say; all I know is that it exists and it becomes available only when a [person] is in that state of mind in which he [or she] knows exactly what he [or she] wants and is fully determined not to quit until he [or she] finds it."[3]

Paul demonstrated tenacity throughout his ministry, but one of the best examples of it came toward the end of his third missionary journey in Asia Minor and Greece. Making his way back to Jerusalem, he sailed from Rhodes and arrived at the port city of Caesarea, where he stayed at the home of Philip, one of seven deacons appointed by the apostles to serve the widows. (See Acts 6.) While there, a prophet named Agabus came to the house, took Paul's belt from him, and bound his own hands and feet to make a point: "Thus says the Holy Spirit, 'This is the way the Jews in Jerusalem will bind the man who owns this belt and will hand him over to the Gentiles'" (Acts 21:11).

All those present took this as a sign that Paul shouldn't go to Jerusalem. After all, how can you argue with the Holy Spirit? But Paul remained resolute in his plans. "What are you doing, weeping and breaking my heart?" he asked. "For I am ready not only to be bound but even to die in Jerusalem for the Lord Jesus." The episode ends with these words, "Since he would not be persuaded, we remained silent except to say, 'The Lord's will be done'" (21:13-14).

No one debates whether the prophet's sign comes from the Holy Spirit. They also seem to agree on the truth of the sign: If Paul goes to Jerusalem he will face arrest and be bound. But over the protests of those gathered, Paul appears to have made peace with this possibility. He doesn't take such a warning as a sign to change course but to get ready. Perhaps we could call this Paul's "I am ready to die" speech. He would not be deterred.

I find this story so inspiring at this point in my life because I'm fifty-three years old, about the same age as Paul when he arrives in Caesarea. Certainly Paul has to be growing weary of setbacks. He faced resistance in Pisidian Antioch and was left for dead in Lystra. He managed to escape angry mobs in Damascus, Jerusalem, Iconium, Thessalonica, Corinth, and Ephesus. He was beaten and arrested in Philippi, and he endured squabbles among church leaders for welcoming Gentiles. He'd also been forced to part ways with Barnabas, the man responsible for Paul becoming an apostle, after a heated argument.

While I am not at the end of my career, I have days when I grow weary from ministry. Another squabble over a seemingly senseless matter, a member leaving the congregation because he or she "doesn't like the direction the church is going," community resistance to a soup kitchen, a complaint over lack of attention from the pastor in a time of need. I don't face being thrown in jail or having people beat me within an inch of my life, but these instances take a toll. Some days I find myself wondering, *How much do I really have left?*

Can you relate? In your call, in your place of service, in your pursuit to follow God's direction in life, do you ever feel like the road is too long and steep? That the wear and tear has worn and torn? It's not simply that your energy wanes or your stamina decreases—it's a more serious symptom. Your heart has begun to check out. Your passion seems to be fading. It's not that you can't continue; you're not sure you care to continue.

This is why I find this story about Paul so encouraging. With all he has endured, signs of a setback ahead do not dissuade him. What keeps Paul going? What keeps his passion strong? What enables him to say, "I am ready not only to be bound but even to die in Jerusalem for the Lord Jesus"?

STAY IN TOUCH WITH YOUR FIRST LOVE

Paul keeps his spiritual ears trained toward heaven. He listens intently for God's voice and remains obedient to God's instructions. Shortly before his arrival in Caesarea, Paul offers a telling statement about his resolve when he addresses the leaders of the Ephesus congregation:

> And now, as a captive to the Spirit, I am on my way to Jerusalem, not knowing what will happen to me there, except that the Holy Spirit testifies to me in every city that imprisonment and persecutions are waiting for me. But I do not count my life of any value to myself, if only I may finish my course and the ministry that I received from the Lord Jesus, to testify to the good news of God's grace. (Acts 20:22-24)

Agabus's demonstration in Caesarea seems to confirm Paul's expectations. Still, knowing that more challenges lie ahead is one thing, but having the tenacity to face them is another. How does Paul steel his resolve? Surely the answer lies in the second part of his statement to the Ephesians. Paul derives his life's worth from following Jesus' call. His embrace of that original call keeps him from getting distracted by other voices or obstacles.

The Ephesus church appears again in the book of Revelation in a way that reinforces this message. While the angel commends the members of the congregation for their ability to endure and not grow weary, the praise comes with a warning: "You have abandoned the love you had at first" (Rev. 2:4). Preventing weariness, the warning seems to say, relates directly to staying in touch with what first moved your heart in ministry.

Sometimes in my role as a pastor, the demands and administration of ministry distract me. Raising money, overseeing building concerns, creating reports, and even the routine grind of sermon writing and teaching can wear me down. At other times, conflicts, disappointments, and challenges can sap my energy and motivation. Every now and then I have to get in touch with the first love that sparked my initial call to ministry.

Just days ago I felt the need to make a number of pastoral visits that I'd put off during the week because of other demands. I carved out a few hours on Saturday when I wasn't missing time with my family. I first went to see a church member dying of cancer. Her son was getting married that weekend in California, but her illness had prevented her attending the ceremony. Her husband loaded his wife and me into a golf cart and drove us to a hilltop overlooking their farm. We sat in the gentle breeze and talked about life and death and what it meant to believe in God.

From there I visited a retired basketball coach who was awaiting surgery for a condition that had left him bedridden. I listened to lively stories from his coaching days and prayed with him about his upcoming surgery.

Then I went to see a woman who had experienced a terrible fall months before and was still finding it difficult to stand even after months of physical therapy. I arrived as her husband attempted to help her to her feet. Together we assisted her until she stood on her own, and then we cheered just as her parents probably did the day she took her first baby steps.

I went home with a lighter heart. Instead of feeling tired, I had new energy. I had offered myself as a vehicle of God's grace and found encouragement in the process. Don't get me wrong. My mood didn't mean that what I do most days is in conflict with my call. Not at all! I just needed to get close to the difference my day-to-day work makes. I had to be revived in *why* I do what I do.

Where are you searching for that *why* in your own life? Maybe you remember your first love of volunteering to help children learn to read, but your involvement has placed you in roles where committee meetings and organizational chores have depleted you. Yes, that nuts-and-bolts work is significant, and it may even be the very thing God has called you to do. But every now and then it's good to reclaim that first love—to sit with a child and read a book together.

Sometimes, though, a sagging heart serves to warn us that we aren't where we should be. Well-intentioned people may have steered us in directions that don't line up well with our gifts and passions. Returning to that first love can sometimes help us sort out whether we are in the right place.

In living out your purpose, what is your first love? What do you remember doing when you felt that initial surge of energy that comes in knowing God is using you?

Lean into Your Faith

Tenacity requires leaning into our faith. I know that sounds spiritually simplistic, but let's pause to understand what builds faith. Søren Kierkegaard wrote of the leap of faith. But with all due respect to the Danish philosopher, faith is not always a blind leap into an unknown future.[4] Faith is also about looking back into a known past and claiming God's hand at work. To be sure, every new challenge requires new faith, but what helps build that faith? I believe new faith comes from understanding and believing how God has worked through previous challenges and obstacles.

Paul has the hindsight of understanding how an imprisonment in Philippi led a jailer and his family to faith. His dispute with Barnabas led to the gospel's being advanced in two directions. Now Paul wants to take the gospel to Rome, the seat of world power. Perhaps he figures that if being in chains provides his ticket there, he stands ready to book passage. When you lean into your faith, you acknowledge that nothing prevents God's purpose from prevailing and that God is still on the job!

United Methodist deacon Reed Hoppe tells the story about a remote region of northern India where Christianity has improbably spread. The reason, Hoppe found out from a missionary friend in the area, is the impact of one man.[5]

Many generations ago, this missionary came to spread the gospel among a society of headhunters. In this culture, boys enter manhood when they kill a warrior in another village and return to their own village with body parts as trophies.

Because the missionary wasn't a warrior, he presented no threat to the village he entered. Though the residents did their best to run him off, he wouldn't go. At one point, the elders even locked him in a cage, thinking he would flee once they released him. Instead he left the village—only to return with his wife!

Throughout his years of ministry, this missionary drew only one member of the tribe into Christian faith. That person, however, turned out to be a great evangelist. Entire villages came to faith through the ministry of this one man, a former headhunter.

"That lone missionary was ignored, harassed, and put into a cage, but he never gave up," Hoppe writes.

Tenacity is powered by the belief that while we may not see the difference we are making at the time, one day we will. One day we will have the best hindsight of all. We will see from the heights of heaven and know exactly how God used our tenacious acts of faith.

RELY ON COMMUNITY

Paul seldom travels alone. We receive occasional glimpses of his entourage. For example, on his third missionary journey that eventually takes him to Caesarea we learn the following:

[Paul] was accompanied by Sopater son of Pyrrhus from Beroea, by Aristarchus and Secundus from Thessalonica, by Gaius from

Derbe, and by Timothy, as well as by Tychicus and Trophimus from Asia. They went ahead and were waiting for us in Troas. (Acts 20:4-5)

Notice beyond all the names, the "us." Along with Luke, author of Acts, even more people come along for the journey. It reminds us that accomplishing anything significant in life requires support. Equally important to what we are doing is whom we are doing it with. We can all get tired and grow weary. We may feel like giving up at times. Perhaps Paul never quits because he surrounds himself with friends, allies, and supporters.

A powerful story of this truth comes to us from the days of the civil rights struggle. In September 1966, Martin Luther King Jr. fell into a bout of deep despair. With the Vietnam war and the space race preoccupying the nation, some feared that the civil rights cause was losing steam. Newspapers even speculated that the efforts had been ineffective. For a period of time King could hardly bring himself to get out of bed.[6]

REMEMBER YOUR SPIRITUAL DNA

Paul refers several times to critical encounters with God. In Second Corinthians he cryptically describes "a person in Christ" who is caught up to "the third heaven" (12:2). Many commentators believe Paul is describing himself in a place of rare connection to God, and I interpret the passage through that lens as well. Paul goes on to say that the man "heard things" from God too secret to repeat (12:4), but what he heard encouraged him to overcome trials and keep persevering.

If Paul is actually talking about himself, I can imagine what he might have heard from God: *Remember who you are. I made you with a determined spirit. Look at all you have done. Recall the challenges and difficulties I have seen you through. You are no quitter. You are a fighter. So keep fighting, and don't quit until I say so.*

That message doesn't require too much imagination. Paul is a determined, ambitious, strong-willed person—both as a Pharisee and as an apostle. He probably drives his companions crazy at times, while at other times he leaves them wondering who but Paul could have accomplished what he has. I picture Paul reinforcing himself with reminders that he's tough; he's not alone. Telling himself: *I have the help of the Holy Spirit. I can do this!*

A heartwarming scene toward the end of the movie *Remember the Titans* takes place between Coach Boone and his wife. He has just found out before the state championship that his key All-American player has been left paralyzed after a car accident. Despite all the challenges he's withstood while coaching the first football team of a newly integrated high school amid serious racial tensions, he now questions himself and the pursuit of his goals. Alone with his wife, he asks, "You think I was blinded by my own ambition?" She replies, "Whatever kind of ambition it took to do what you did around here, this world could use a lot more of it."[7] Sometimes those around us offer reminders of who we are and the difference we make.

I call this remembering our spiritual DNA. It's not just recalling our positive traits or successful endeavors. It's claiming how God uses—and will continue to use—who we are.

The name Saul means "prayed for." The name Paul means "humble." Perhaps Paul remembered who he was by holding on to an identity marked by humble reliance on God.

There's a power in naming. When Australian tennis coach Harry Hopman took on a slow-footed player with potential, he employed a creative motivational technique. He nicknamed the player "Rocket." "Rocket Rod" Laver went on to become an international tennis champion. Perhaps hearing someone constantly shout "Rocket" helped him believe who he could be.[8]

If you were to give yourself a spiritual name what would it be? *Semper Fi* (always faithful) Steve? Joyful Janet? Miracle Worker Mark? Laurie the Leader?

Me? I am Relentless Rob!

At this point, knowing our spiritual history helps us. When you feel distressed because friends and enemies alike have turned against you, remember David who "strengthened himself in the LORD his God" even in the midst of a popular uprising (1 Sam. 30:6). When you get exhausted and want to quit, remember Elijah who thought he was forsaken in the wilderness only to be restored by God (1 Kings 19). When your failure causes you to give up on yourself, remember Jesus' appearing to a dejected Peter by the lakeshore and encouraging him three times to "feed my sheep" (John 21). These aren't just historical stories; they are our stories. They represent our spiritual DNA. God pledges to all of us the help that these biblical figures received. We do not recollect what God once did; we accept the promise of what God will do.

As God once reminded Moses when Moses suffered from dejection, "Is [my] power limited?" (Num. 11:23). We call upon this same strength when we sing the hymn "Leaning on the Everlasting Arms."

Sometimes in discouragement, I turn to a popular poem of unknown authorship called "Don't Quit." While not overtly spiritual in nature, it speaks to the power and importance of tenacity. I believe the poem characterizes Paul and encourages us to remain steadfast:

> When things go wrong, as they sometimes will,
> When the road you're trudging seems all uphill,
> When the funds are low and the debts are high,
> And you want to smile, but you have to sigh,
> When care's pressing you down a bit—
> Rest if you must, but don't you quit.

Life is queer with its twists and turns,
As every one of us sometimes learns,
And many a person turns about
When they might have won had they stuck it out.
Don't give up though the pace seems slow—
You may succeed with another blow.

Often the goal is nearer than
It seems to a faint and faltering man;
Often the strugglers have given up
When they might have captured the victor's cup;
And learned too late when the night came down
How close they were to the golden crown.

Success is failure turned inside out—
The silver tint of the clouds of doubt
And you never can tell how close you are,
It may be near when it seems afar;
So stick to the fight when you're hardest hit—
It's when things seem worst that you mustn't quit.[9]

Agabus's warning turns out to be true. Paul is arrested in Jerusalem and stands trial several times before the Jewish council, known as the Sanhedrin, as well as before various Roman officials. He appeals to Caesar, and after spending more than two years in prison, he finally sails for Rome, a trip that takes almost six months. Along the way he survives shipwrecks and snakebite. He finally arrives in Rome, and there he meets his death.

Today, a few miles from the center of Rome, is the Basilica of St. Paul. Beneath the altar is a sarcophagus believed to contain the remains of Paul. A large statue of Paul holding a sword over one shoulder stands in front of the entrance to the basilica. At first glance, it seems an odd way to portray Paul, since there is no mention of his carrying a sword in his travels. But tradition holds that Paul's martyrdom came through beheading, and artisans often depicted the manner in which their subjects died.

We don't know for sure how or when Paul died. The book of Acts closes with Paul under house arrest. He still receives visitors and answers the call that came with his conversion to Christ: He "welcomed all who came to him, proclaiming the kingdom of God and teaching about the Lord Jesus Christ with all boldness and without hindrance" (Acts 28:30-31).

Paul was faithful to the end. I pray you will be too.

SERVANT SPOTLIGHT

Sister Marie Simone Achille Tells Her Story

In 1987 I attended a workshop on education in Port au Prince, Haiti. While there, a priest named Father Joseph Phillipe asked for a volunteer to help him start a school in his hometown of Fondwa. Intrigued, I raised my hand. For thirty years I have never looked back with regret on my decision and how God brought me to this small, beautiful, and impoverished village in Haiti.

I began the Sainte Antoine School in a dilapidated barn. While starting Fondwa's first learning center, I also cared for orphaned children, providing a stable home, sound nutrition, and a well-rounded education. In need of more people to help me, I began the Order of the Sisters of St. Antoine with another nun named Sister Carmelle Voltaire. Together, this ministry has grown into a thriving community that offers hope and help to hundreds of children and families. Yet, it has not happened without challenges.

The massive earthquake in 2010 created a crisis in the community. The school collapsed. The orphanage sustained damage that rendered it uninhabitable. Most families we serve lost everything they had. Hundreds died. Trying to continue routine work while attending four or more funerals a day, ministering to families in overwhelming grief, and having little or no resources with which to face the unimaginable loss left me discouraged. But I was not defeated!

I was back to living in a barn—only this time with fifty-five children! The school continued just as it started: in makeshift stalls. I prayed. I believed that God would not leave us in the rubble. The support of the other sisters and partner churches in the United States kept us going. Some days I felt God saying to me, "Sister Simone, look around you. All these children depend on you. Now you depend on me, and together we will get the work done!"

Today, the new St. Antoine School is more beautiful than anything I could have imagined. The new Fatima Orphanage is nearly finished with the upgrades of indoor plumbing and treated water. The children are witnessing firsthand what life can be when you do not allow tragedy to have the final word and you never take no for an answer.

REFLECTION QUESTIONS

• When in your call, in your place of service, in your pursuit to follow God's direction in life, have you felt like the road is just too long and steep?

• What helps you persevere?

• What do you remember doing when you felt that initial surge of energy that comes in knowing that God is using you?

• How do you build your faith?

• How do you find support in community?

• What is your spiritual DNA?

ACKNOWLEDGMENTS

Undertaking this book project set me on my own spiritual journey, and I couldn't have completed it without a circle of support that's both wide and strong.

I first want to express my enormous gratitude to the staff of The Upper Room, particularly Betsy Hall, whose steady hand shepherded the entire project, and Sherry Elliott, who signed on for the adventure of overseeing the video-production logistics in Turkey, Israel, and Greece. I will forever cherish our memories of 2 a.m. rides to hotels and sitting in sidewalk cafes in such remote and historic locations.

Nancy Kruh also deserves my thanks for her editorial finesse and enthusiasm; her wise counsel in content suggestions proved invaluable. Pauline scholar Jeremy Bakker offered me a wealth of insights at the start, as well as a keen eye and helpful advice during the writing and editing process.

Thanks also go to principal videographer James Hutcheson and photographer Jon Woon, both dedicated followers of Christ. Their creativity and high standard of excellence are evident in every aspect of the videos. On the back end, Matthew Pessoni and Gemini

Production Group, Inc., contributed excellent editing and sharp production work.

I'm grateful, as well, to the faithful congregation and tremendous staff at St. Luke's United Methodist Church in Indianapolis. Their unflagging support afforded me the time to write and travel for this project.

As always, I cannot say enough about my executive assistant, Marsha Thompson, who helped with travel arrangements, schedule coordination, and research. Marsha is one of the most servant-hearted people I know, and it is a gift to work with her every day.

I particularly want to single out the almost eighty St. Luke's members who were on the "Travels of Paul" tour when I did much of the filming. Thanks for your understanding on those days when I had to dash off to a shoot! I especially appreciate all the work of member Bob Zehr who coordinated the group's trip and went the extra mile to accommodate my travel and schedule needs.

I couldn't have undertaken this project without the enormous influence of the late Dr. Fred Craddock, my preaching professor and academic advisor in seminary. He was the one who inspired in me a desire to learn and an appreciation of Paul's life and letters. He planted the seeds of my understanding of Paul as a flesh-and-blood man. Dr. Craddock's writing and teaching continue to challenge me to live a purposeful life.

I save my final words for my wife, Susan, who is the one who keeps nudging me on a daily basis to explore my purpose in life. From practically the moment we met, we have shared each other's calls and have sought to support each other in following God's direction for our lives. I am indebted to the gifts of patience, judgment, and counsel that she has offered so generously to me during this project and throughout my ministry.

NOTES

INTRODUCTION: LOCATING YOUR STARTING POINT

Epigraph: Translated from D. Martin Luther's *Werke, Kritische Gesamtausgabe* (Weimarer Ausgabe), Volume 42: *Genesisvorlesung (Cap. 1–17)*, ed. Karl Drescher (Weimar: H. Böhlau, 1911), 98.

1. Philip Wingeier-Rayo, "John Wesley's Missiology: A Review of Moravian Contributions." Paper presented to the Mission and Evangelism Working Group, Twelfth Oxford Institute of Methodist Theological Studies, Durham, NC, August 12–21, 2007, 6–12. [oimts.files.wordpress.com/2013/04/2007-5-wingeier-rayo.pdf]

2. John Wesley, eds. W. Reginald Ward and Richard P. Heitzenrater, vol. 18, *The Bicentennial Edition of the Works of John Wesley* (Nashville, TN: Abingdon Press, 1976), 142–43.

3. Ibid., 145–46.

4. Ibid., 249–50.

1 PREPARING FOR PURPOSE

Epigraph: Greg Anderson, *Living Life on Purpose: A Guide to Creating a Life of Success and Significance* (San Francisco, CA: Harper, 1997), 12.

1. Matthew L. Wald, "Safety Board Blames Pilot Error in Crash of Kennedy Plane," the website of the *New York Times* (nytimes.com), posted July 7, 2000.

2. Melanie Standish and Dan Witters, "World Faces Shortage in Purpose Well-Being," the website of Gallup, Inc. (gallup.com), posted September 23, 2014.

3. Susan Adams, "Most Americans Are Unhappy at Work," the website of *Forbes Magazine* (forbes.com), posted June 20, 2014.

4. Emily Esfahani Smith, "There's More to Life Than Being Happy: Meaning Comes from the Pursuit of More Complex Things Than Happiness," the website of *Atlantic Monthly* (theatlantic.com), posted January 9, 2013.

5. Os Guinness, *Rising to the Call: Discovering the Ultimate Purpose of Your Life* (Nashville, TN: Thomas Nelson, 2003), xi.

6. Max Lucado, *Cure for the Common Life: Living in Your Sweet Spot* (Nashville, TN: Thomas Nelson, 2005), 18.

7. Adam Hamilton, *The Call: The Life and Message of the Apostle Paul* (Nashville, TN: Abingdon Press, 2015), 26.

8. Paul Tillich, *Systematic Theology*, vol. 2 (Chicago: University of Chicago Press, 1957), 179.

9. Tara Parker-Pope, "Creating a New Mission Statement," Well (blog), the website of the *New York Times* (nytimes.com), posted January 5, 2015 [well.blogs. nytimes.com/2015/01/05/personal-coaches-and-mission-statements/?_r=0].

10. Julius C. Trimble, United Methodist Churches of Indiana official website, accessed September 1, 2016.

2 TAKING STOCK

Epigraph: Os Guinness, *The Call: Finding and Fulfilling the Central Purpose of Your Life* (Nashville, TN: Word, 1998), 46.

1. David Woods, "Hiring a young Stevens pays for Butler," the website of the *Indianapolis Star* (www.indystar.com), posted March 30, 2010.

2. Bruce Feiler, "The Stories That Bind Us," *New York Times*, page ST1, March 15, 2013.

3. Robert Isaac Wilberforce and Samuel Wilberforce, *The Correspondence of William Wilberforce*, two volumes (London: John Murray, Albermarle Street, 1840), 1.56.

4. Daisy Fuentes, "A Place of Hope: Daisy Fuentes Finds New Hope during a Visit to St. Jude Children's Hospital," *Guideposts*, May 2011, 34–38.

3   FACING ADVERSITY

Epigraphs: G. K. Chesterton, *What's Wrong with the World* (Pantianos Classics, 1910), 18.

John Ortberg, *All the Places to Go . . . How Will You Know?: God Has Placed before You an Open Door. What Will You Do?* (Carol Stream, IL: Tyndale House Publishers, Inc., 2015), 91.

1. Jim Collins, foreword to *The Daily Drucker: 366 Days of Insight and Motivation for Getting the Right Things Done*, by Peter F. Drucker, (New York: HarperBusiness, 2005), vii–x.

2. Martin Luther King Jr., sermon delivered at Dexter Avenue Baptist Church, Montgomery, AL, November 6, 1956, published in *The Papers of Martin Luther King, Jr.*, vol. vi: Advocate of the Social Gospel, September 1948-March 1963, eds. Clayborne Carson, Susan Carson (Berkeley: University of California Press, 2007), 303.

3. Quoted by J. Ellsworth Kalas in *The Will of God in an Unwilling World* (Louisville, KY: Westminster John Knox, 2011), 61.

4. C. S. Lewis, *The Great Divorce* (New York, NY: MacMillan Publishing Company, 1977), 72.

5 . Jim Cymbala with Dean Merrill, *Fresh Wind, Fresh Fire: What Happens When God's Spirit Invades the Hearts of His People* (Grand Rapids, MI: Zondervan, 2003), 19.

4   DEALING WITH DETOURS

Epigraph: Harry Emerson Fosdick, *Riverside Sermons* (New York, NY: Harper & Brothers, 1958), 54.

1. Dr. David Jeremiah, sermon delivered at Thomas Road Baptist Church, Lynchburg, Virginia, on May 1, 2011.

2. Martin Luther King Jr. interview by Ned Brooks, *Meet the Press*, NBC, April 17, 1960.

3. Houston Bryan Roberson, *Fighting the Good Fight: The Story of the Dexter Avenue King Memorial Baptist Church, 1865–1977* (New York: Routledge, 2005), 116–21.

4. Robert Frost, *Mountain Interval* (New York: Henry Holt and Company, 1916), 9.

5. Kalas, *The Will of God in an Unwilling World*, 61.

6. Frank & Robert Laubach, *Toward World Literacy: The Each One Teach One Way* (Eastford, CT: Martino Fine Books, 2012).

5   RELYING ON GOD

Epigraph: Erich Fromm, *The Sane Society* (Abingdon, England: Routledge & Kegan Paul, 1955), 196.

1. "Olympic Games," *Time*, August 17, 1936: 37.

2. For more detailed information, see Tim Byce, *Morphing into the Real World: The Handbook for Entering the Work Force* (Palm Harbor, Florida: M&JB Investment Company, 2007).

3. Susan Krauss Whitbourne, "4 Signs That Someone Is Probably Insecure," Fulfillment at Any Age (blog), the website of *Psychology Today* (psychologytoday. com), posted November 17, 2015.

6   DEVELOPING TENACITY

1. Nelson Mandela, from prepared speech delivered at Palace of Justice, Pretoria Supreme Court, Pretoria, South Africa, April 20, 1964. http://db.nelsonmandela. org/speeches/pub_view.asp?pg=item&ItemID=NMS010&txtstr=prepared%20 to%20die

2. Michael Trimmer, "Nelson Mandela and His Faith," *Christianity Today* (christianitytoday.com), December 10, 2013. [www.christiantoday.com/article/ nelson.mandela.and.his.faith/34956.htm]

3. Mack R. Douglas, *How to Make a Habit of Succeeding* (Grand Rapids, MI: Zondervan, 1966), 38.

4. Søren Kierkegaard, *Fear and Trembling* (London: Penguin Books Ltd., 1985), 77.

5. Reed Hoppe, "Love God, Love Others, Make Disciples," *Good News Magazine*, July August 2016, 43.

6. Taylor Branch, *At Canaan's Edge: America in the King Years 1965–68* (New York: Simon and Schuster, 2006), 529.

7. *Remember the Titans*. Directed by Boaz Yakin. Burbank, CA: Walt Disney Pictures, 2000.

8. Rod Laver with Bud Collins, *The Education of a Tennis Player* (New York: New Chapter Press, 2010), 35.

9. Ralph J. Sabock, Michael D. Sabock, *Coaching: A Realistic Perspective* (Lanham, MD: Rowman & Littlefield, 2011), 273.

About the Author

Rob Fuquay serves as senior pastor at St. Luke's United Methodist Church in Indianapolis. Before taking this appointment in 2011, he served serveral congregations, both large and small, in his native North Carolina. Rob earned his undergraduate degree from Pfeiffer College (now University) in Misenheimer, North Carolina, and his master of divinity from Candler School of Theology at Emory University in Atlanta. He loves the outdoors and enjoys hiking, climbing, and playing golf. Rob and his wife, Susan, also are sports fans who avidly follow baseball, football, basketball, and auto racing. They are the parents of three daughters, Julie, Sarah, and Anna. Rob's previous study series *The God We Can Know* was released by Upper Room Books in 2014. A second, *Take the Flag*, was released in 2016. To learn more about Rob and his published works, visit RobFuquay.com